PRAISE FOR HENRY /

"Giroux lays out a blistering critique of an America governed by the tenets of a market economy. . . . He cites French philosopher Georges Didi-Huberman's concept of the 'disimagination machine' to describe a culture and pedagogical philosophy that short-circuits citizens' ability to think critically, leaving the generation now reaching adulthood unprepared for an 'inhospitable' world. Picking apart the current malaise of 21st-century digital disorder, Giroux describes a world in which citizenship is replaced by consumerism and the functions of engaged governance are explicitly beholden to corporations."

— *Publishers Weekly*

"In terms that are both eloquent and prophetic, Henry Giroux succeeds in raising the ante in the current debate about America's madness. His concept of disimagination captures the emotional as well as the material dimensions of the Western crisis. Beyond economic distress, Giroux paints a far more comprehensive portrait of the alarming descent into violence that afflicts our societies. Yet, as is Giroux's wont, he does not leave us hanging. The final section of the book is a ringing affirmation of hope and struggle for the revival of the radical imagination."

—Stanley Aronowitz, author of *Taking it Big: C. Wright Mills and the Making of Political Intellectuals*

"One of the twelve Canadians changing the way we think."
—*Toronto Star*

"Once again Henry Giroux shows why he is one of the most important public intellectuals in the world today . . . he positively reinforces his commitment to a critical pedagogy that refuses to accept the inevitability of the abuses of power that appear right before our eyes."
—Brad Evans, founder/director, Histories of Violence Project, University of Bristol

"Henry Giroux is one of our most important public intellectuals. Though he vividly describes the privatization of compassion, the rapid decline of higher education's commitment to democracy and shared notions of the public good, the force of Giroux's writings shows us we are not alone and there is power in his arguments of resistance."
—David H. Price, professor of anthropology, St. Martin's University

The Violence
of Organized Forgetting

THINKING BEYOND AMERICA'S
DISIMAGINATION MACHINE

Henry A. Giroux

Open Media Series | City Lights Books

Copyright © 2014 by Henry A. Giroux
All Rights Reserved

ISBN: 9780872866195

Open Media Series editor: Greg Ruggiero

Cover design by John Yates at Stealworks.com

Library of Congress Cataloging-in-Publication Data
Giroux, Henry A.
The violence of organized forgetting : thinking beyond America's di-
simagination machine / Henry A. Giroux.
    pages cm. — (City lights open media)
Includes bibliographical references and index.
ISBN 978-0-87286-619-5 (paperback)
1. Political culture—United States. 2. Corporate power—United
States. 3. Mass media—Political aspects—United States. 4. Power
(Social sciences)—United States. 5. Social values—Political aspects—
United States. 6. Collective memory—Political aspects—United
States. I. Title.
JK1726.G57 2014
306.20973—dc23
                                    2014006179

City Lights Books are published at the City Lights Bookstore,
261 Columbus Avenue, San Francisco, CA 94133.
www.citylights.com

To Susan, again and again

To Rob, Ray, and Reno, my working-class comrades

Contents

AMERICA'S DESCENT INTO MADNESS

America has entered one of its periods of historical madness, but this is the worst I can remember: worse than McCarthyism, worse than the Bay of Pigs and in the long term potentially more disastrous than the Vietnam war.
                                        —John Le Carré

America is descending into madness. The stories it now tells are filled with cruelty, deceit, lies, and legitimate all manner of corruption and mayhem. The mainstream media spin stories that are largely racist, violent, and irresponsible—stories that celebrate power and demonize victims, all the while camouflaging their pedagogical influence under the glossy veneer of entertainment. Violence now offers the only currency with any enduring value for mediating relationships, addressing problems, or offering instant pleasure. A predatory culture celebrates a narcissistic hyper-individualism that radiates a near sociopathic lack of interest in—or compassion and responsibility for—others. Anti-public intellectuals who dominate the screen and aural cultures urge us to spend more, indulge more, and make a virtue out of the pursuit of personal gain, while producing a depoliticized culture of consumerism. Undermining life-affirming social solidarities and any viable notion of the public good, politicians trade in forms of idiocy and superstition that seem to mesmerize the undereducated and render the thoughtful cynical and disengaged. Militarized police forces armed with the latest weapons tested in Afghanistan and Iraq play out their fantasies on the home front by forming robo-SWAT teams that willfully assault protesters and raid neighborhood poker games.[1] Congressional lobbyists hired by big corporations and defense contractors create conditions in which war zones abroad can be re-created at home in order to market military-grade surveillance tools and weapons to a full range of clients, from gated communities to privately owned for-profit prisons.

The stories we tell about ourselves no longer speak to the ideals of justice, equality, liberty, and democracy. The landscape of American politics no longer features towering figures such as Martin Luther King Jr., whose stories interwove moral outrage with courage and vision and inspired us to imagine a society that was never just enough. A culture that once opened our imagination now disables it, overwhelming the populace with nonstop marketing that reduces our sense of agency to the imperatives of ownership, shopping, credit, and debt. But these are not the only narratives that diminish our capacity to imagine a better world. We are also inundated with stories of cruelty and fear that undermine communal bonds and tarnish any viable visions of the future. Different stories, ones that provided a sense of history, social responsibility, and respect for the public good, were once circulated by our parents, religious institutions, schools, and community leaders. Today, the stories that define who we are as individuals and as a nation are manufactured by corporate media that broadcast the lifestyles of celebrities, billionaires, and ethically frozen politicians who preach the mutually related virtues of an unbridled free market and a permanent war economy. The power to reimagine, doubt, and think critically no longer seem possible in a society in which self-interest has become the "only motive force in human life and competition" and "the most efficient and socially beneficial way for that force to express itself."[2]

These stories reciting the neoliberal gospel are all the more powerful because they seem to defy the public's desire for rigorous accountability, critical interrogation, and openness as they generate employment and revenue for right-wing think tanks and policy makers who rush to satisfy the content dictates of corporate media advertisers. Concealing the conditions of their own making, these stories enshrine both greed and indifference, encouraging massive disparities in wealth, health, nutrition, education, housing, and debt. In addition, they sanctify the workings of the market, forging a new political theology that inscribes a sense of our collective destiny to be governed ultimately and exclusively by market forces. Such ideas surely signal a tribute to Ayn Rand's dystopian society, if not also a rebirth of Margaret Thatcher's nonfiction invocation of the mantra of the wealthy: there is nothing beyond individual gain and the values of the corporate order.

The stories that now dominate the American landscape, and of which I write in the following pages, embody what stands for common sense among market and religious fundamentalists in both mainstream political parties: shock-and-awe austerity measures; tax cuts that serve the rich and powerful and destroy government programs that help the disadvantaged, elderly, and sick; attacks on women's reproductive rights; attempts to suppress voter-ID laws and rig electoral college votes; full-fledged assaults on the environment; the militarization of everyday life; the destruction of public education, if not critical thought itself; and an ongoing attack on unions, social provisions, and the expansion of Medicaid and meaningful health care reform. These stories are endless, repeated by the neoliberal and neoconservative walking dead who roam the planet sucking the blood and life out of everyone they touch—from the millions killed in foreign wars to the millions at home forced into underemployment, foreclosure, poverty, or prison.

All of these stories embody what Ernst Bloch has called "the swindle of fulfillment."[3] That is, instead of fostering a democracy rooted in the public interest, they encourage a political and economic system controlled by the rich but carefully packaged in a consumerist and militarist fantasy. Instead of promoting a society that embraces a robust and inclusive social contract, they legitimate a social order that shreds social protections, privileges the wealthy and powerful, and inflicts a maddening and devastating set of injuries upon workers, women, poor minorities, immigrants, and low- and middle-class young people. Instead of striving for economic and political stability, they impose on Americans already marginalized by class and race uncertainty and precarity, a world turned upside-down, in which ignorance becomes a virtue and power and wealth are utilized for ruthlessness and privilege rather than a resource for the public good.

Every once in a while we catch a brutal glimpse of what America has become in the narratives spun by politicians and corporate elite whose arrogance and quests for authority exceed their interest to conceal the narrow-mindedness, power-hungry blunders, cruelty, and hardship embedded in the policies they advocate. The echoes of a culture of cruelty can be heard in politicians such as Senator Tom A. Coburn, a Republican from Oklahoma, who believes that social assistance to those in need of a place to live, work, or more equitable salaries should be cut in the name of austerity measures. We hear it in the words of Representative Mike Reynolds, another Republican from Oklahoma, who insists that government bears no responsibility to improve access to college education through a state program "that provides post-secondary education scholarships to qualified low-income students."[4] We see evidence of the culture of cruelty in the policies of liberal and right-wing politicians who refuse to extend unemployment benefits, have cut $8 billion from the food stamp program (SNAP), which primarily benefits children, and have opted out of Medicaid expansion. These decisions will be deeply consequential. A Harvard University and CUNY study . . . found that the lack of Medicaid expansion in these opt-out states will result in about 7,000 to 17,000 deaths a year.[5] Similar indications of the culture of cruelty are on display in the call on the part of right-wing billionaire Charles Koch who reaps billions of dollars yearly from his investments while simultaneously calling for the abolition of the minimum wage.[6] We find evidence of a savage culture of cruelty in numerous policies that make clear that those who occupy the most marginalized sectors of American society—whether low-income families, communities of color, or young, unemployed, and failed consumers—are considered entirely disposable in terms of ethical considerations and the "grammar of human suffering."[7]

In the name of austerity, budget cuts are enacted and fall primarily on those individuals and groups who are already disenfranchised, and will thus seriously worsen the lives of those people now suffering the most. For instance, Governor Rick Perry of Texas has enacted legislation that refuses state participation in the Obama administration's Medicaid expansion; as a result, health care coverage will be denied to over 1.5 million low-income residents of Texas.[8] This is not merely partisan politics. It is an expression of a new form of savagery and barbarism aimed at those now considered disposable in a market-centered society that has embraced a neo-Darwinian survival-of-the-fittest mentality. Not surprisingly, the right-wing appeal to job-killing and provision-slashing now functions as an updated form of medieval torture, gutting a myriad of programs that will quickly add up to profound suffering for the many and benefits for only a small class of predatory bankers, hedge-fund managers, and financiers who leech off society.

The general response from progressives and liberals

does not take seriously the ways in which the extreme right wing articulates its increasingly pervasive and destructive view of American society. For instance, the proposals of the new extremists in Congress are often treated, especially by liberals, as cruel hoaxes that are out of touch with reality or as foolhardy attempts to roll back the Obama agenda. On the left, such views tend to be criticized as a domestic version of the tactics employed by the Taliban—keeping people uneducated and ignorant, oppressing women, living in a circle of certainty, and turning all channels of information into a mass propaganda machine of fundamentalist Americanism.[9] All of these critiques take aim at a deeply authoritarian agenda. But such commentaries do not go far enough. Tea Party politics are about more than bad policy and policies that favor the rich over the poor, or for that matter about modes of governance and ideology that represent a blend of civic and moral turpitude. In this instance, the hidden political order represents the poison of neoliberalism and its ongoing attempt to destroy those very institutions whose purpose is to enrich public memory, decrease human suffering, protect the environment, distribute social provisions, and safeguard the public good. Neoliberalism, or what can be called the latest stage of predatory capitalism, is part of a broader project of restoring class power and consolidating the rapid concentration of capital. It is a political, economic, and political project that constitutes an ideology, mode of governance, policy, and form of public pedagogy. As an ideology, it construes profit making as the essence of democracy, consuming as the only operable form of citizenship, and an irrational assertion that the market both solves all problems and serves as a model for structuring all social relations.

As a mode of governance, neoliberalism imposes identities, subjects, and ways of life detached from civic accountability and government regulations. Driven by a survival-of-the-fittest ethic, neoliberal practices buy into the rights and privileges of business and private ownership and are removed from matters of ethics and social costs. As a political project, neoliberalism is wedded to the privatization of all public resources, the selling off of state holdings and functions, the deregulation of finance and labor, the elimination of welfare and unions, the deregulation of trade in goods and capital investment, and the marketization, commercialization, and commodification of all aspects of everyday life.

Neoliberalism creates a political landscape devoid of public accountability, access, and agency, which is to say devoid of democracy itself. As a predatory competition for hoarding profit, neoliberalism produces massive inequality in wealth and income, shifts political power to financial elites, destroys all vestiges of the social contract, and increasingly views "unproductive" sectors—most often those marginalized by race, class, disability, resident status, and age—as suspicious, potentially criminal, and ultimately disposable. It thus criminalizes social problems and manufactures profit by commercializing surveillance, policing, and prisons.

The views and concerns of elite private privilege and competitive ownership now out-compete and replace notions of the public good, civic community, and solidarity. Under neoliberalism the social is pathologized while violence and war are normalized, packaged and marketed as cartoons, video games, television, cinema, and other highly profitable entertainment products. Neoliberalism indebts the public to feed the profits of the rich by spending obscene amounts on militarization, surveillance, and war. In the end, it becomes a virulent antagonist to the very institutions meant to eliminate human suffering, protect the environment, uphold the right of unions, and provide resources for those in need. As a rival to egalitarianism and the public good, neoliberalism has no real solutions to the host of economic, political, and social problems generated as its by-products.

At the heart of neoliberal narratives is a disimagination machine that spews out stories inculcating a disdain for community, public values, public life, and democracy itself. Celebrated instead are pathological varieties of individualism, distorted notions of freedom, and a willingness to employ state violence to suppress dissent and abandon those suffering from a collection of social problems ranging from chronic impoverishment and joblessness to homelessness. Within this rationality, markets are not merely freed from progressive government regulation—they are removed from any considerations of social costs. And even where government regulation does exist, it functions primarily to bail out the rich and shore up collapsing financial institutions, working for what Noam Chomsky has termed America's only political party, "the business party."[10] The stories that attempt to cover up America's embrace of historical and social amnesia at the same time justify authoritarianism with a soft edge and weaken democracy through a thousand cuts to the body politic. How else to explain the Obama administration's willingness to assassinate U.S. citizens suspected of associating with outlaw groups and to secretly monitor the email messages, phone calls, Internet activity, and text messages of its citizens? Or to use the National Defense Authorization Act (NDAA) to arrest and indefinitely detain U.S. citizens without charge or trial, maintain an unjust military tribunal system, and use drones as part of a global assassination campaign to kill not just people suspected of crimes but also any innocent person who happens to be nearby when these weapons detonate near them? As Jonathan Turley points out: "An authoritarian nation is defined not just by the use of authoritarian powers, but by the ability to use them. If a president can take away your freedom or your life on his own authority, all rights become little more than a discretionary grant subject to executive will." [11]

Ultimately, these acts of abuse and aggression offer evidence of a new reality emerging in the United States that enshrines a politics of disposability, in which growing numbers of people are considered to be a dispensable drain on the economy and thus an affront to the sensibilities of the rich and powerful. Rather than work for a more dignified life, most Americans now work simply to get by in a survival-of-the-fittest society in which getting ahead and accumulating property and power, especially for the ruling elite, is the only game in town. In the past, public values have been challenged and certain groups have been targeted as superfluous or redundant. But what is new about the politics of disposability that has become a central feature of contemporary American politics is the way in which such antidemocratic practices have become normalized in the existing neoliberal order. A politics of inequality and ruthless power disparities is now matched by a culture of cruelty defined by the slow violence of debt, impoverishment, wartime military recruitment, criminalization, incarceration, and silent misery. Private injuries not only are separated from public considerations, but historical narratives of structural impoverishment and exclusion are ignored, scorned, or simply censored, as they are in states like Arizona that have forbidden books by Mumia Abu-Jamal, Howard Zinn, and Winona LaDuke from public schools.[12] Similarly, all noncommercial public spheres where such stories might be shared are viewed with contempt, a perfect supplement to the chilling indifference to the plight of communities who are disadvantaged, disenfranchised, and preyed upon. There is a particularly savage violence in the stories that now shape matters of governance, policy, education, and everyday life, one that has made America barely recognizable as a civilian democracy.

Any viable struggle against the authoritarian forces that dominate the United States must make visible the indignity and injustice of these narratives and the historical, political, economic, and cultural conditions that produce them. For this reason, in *The Violence of Organized Forgetting* I present a critical analysis of how various elitist forces in American society are distracting, miseducating, and deterring the public from acting in its own interests. Dominant political and cultural responses to current events—such as the ongoing economic crisis; income inequality, health care reform, Hurricane Sandy, the war on terror, the Boston Marathon bombing, Edward Snowden's exposure of the gross misdeeds of the National Security Agency, and the crisis of public schooling—represent flashpoints that reveal a growing disregard for people's democratic rights, public accountability, and civic values. As political power becomes increasingly disconnected from civic, ethical, and material moorings, it becomes easier to punish and imprison young people than to educate them.

From the inflated rhetoric of the political right to market-driven media peddling spectacles of violence, the influence of these criminogenic and death-dealing forces is undermining our collective security by justifying cutbacks to social services and suppressing opportunities for democratic resistance. Saturating mainstream discourses with anti-public narratives, the neoliberal machinery of civic death effectively weakens public supports and prevents the emergence of much-needed new ways of thinking and speaking about politics in the twenty-first century. But even more than neutralizing all forms of viable opposition to the growing control and wealth of predatory financial elites, responses to social issues are increasingly dominated by a malignant characterization of disadvantaged groups as disposable populations. How else to explain the right-wing charge that the poor, disabled, sick, and elderly are moochers and should fend for themselves? This is not simply an example of a kind of hardening of the culture, it is also part of a machinery of social and civic death that crushes any viable notion of the common good, public life, and the shared bonds and commitments that are necessary for community and democracy.

Before this dangerously authoritarian mind-set has a chance to take hold of our collective imagination and animate our social institutions, it is crucial that all Americans think critically and ethically about the coercive forces shaping U.S. culture—and focus our energy on what can be done to change them. It is not enough for people of conscience only to expose the falseness of the stories we are told. Educators, artists, intellectuals, workers, young people, and other concerned citizens also need to create alternative narratives about what the promise of democracy might be for our communities and ourselves. This demands a break from established political parties, the creation of alternative public spheres in which to produce democratic narratives and visions, and a notion of politics that is educative, one that takes seriously how people interpret and mediate the world, how they see themselves in relation to others, and what it might mean *to imagine* otherwise in order *to act* otherwise. Why are not millions protesting in the streets over these barbaric policies that deprive them of life, liberty, justice, equality, and dignity? What are the pedagogical technologies and practices at work that create the conditions for people to act against their own sense of dignity, agency, and collective possibilities? Progressives and others need to make education central to any viable sense of politics so as to make matters of memory, imagination, and consciousness central elements of what it means to be critical and engaged citizens.

The American public needs more than a show of outrage or endless demonstrations. It needs to develop a formative culture for producing a language of critique, possibility, and broad-based political change. Such a project is indispensable for developing an organized politics that speaks to a future that can secure a dignified life for all: living wages, safe housing, educational opportunities, a sustainable environment, and public support for the arts and other forms of cultural enrichment, particularly for young people. At stake here is a politics and vision that informs ongoing educational and political struggles to awaken the inhabitants of neoliberal societies to their current reality and what it means to be educated not only to think outside of a ruthless market-driven rationality but also to struggle for those values, hopes, modes of solidarity, power relations, and institutions that infuse democracy with a spirit of egalitarianism and economic and social justice.

The Violence of Organized Forgetting not only demonstrates the ways in which America is under siege by forms of political extremism but also explains how too many progressives are stuck in a discourse of foreclosure and disaster and instead need to develop what Stuart Hall called a "sense of politics being educative, of politics changing the way people see things."[13] This is a difficult task, but what we are seeing in cities around the world is the need for the confluence of new and indigenous forms of resistance, a new vision of politics, and a renewed hope in collective struggles and the development of broad-based organizations, all of which are central in the struggle for a substantive democracy. This is a challenge for young people and all those invested in the promise of a democracy to transform the meaning of politics through a commitment to economic justice and democratic social change.

The issues of who gets to define the future, own the nation's wealth, shape the reach of state resources, control the global flow of goods and humans, and invest in institutions that educate an engaged and socially responsible citizenry have become largely invisible. And yet these are precisely the issues that must be confronted in order to address how matters of representation, education, economic justice, and politics are to be defined and fought over. The stories told by corporate liars and crooks do serious harm to the body politic, and the damage they cause together with the idiocy they reinforce are becoming more apparent as America becomes increasingly pliant to authoritarianism and the relentless ambient influences of manufactured fear and commercial entertainment that support it.

There is a need for social movements that invoke stories as a form of public memory, stories that have the potential to unsettle common sense, challenge the commonplace, and move communities to invest in their own sense of civic and collective agency. Such stories make knowledge meaningful in order to make it critical and transformative and provide a different sense of how the world is narrated. These are moments of pedagogical and political grace.[14] As Kristen Case argues: "There is difficulty, discomfort, even fear in such moments, which involve confrontations with what we thought we knew, like why people have mortgages and what 'things' are. These moments do not reflect a linear progress from ignorance to knowledge; instead they describe a step away from a complacent knowing into a new world in which, at least at first, everything is cloudy, nothing is quite clear."[15] She continues: "We cannot be a democracy if this power [to imagine otherwise] is allowed to become a luxury commodity."[16] If democracy is to once again inspire a populist politics, it is crucial to develop a number of social movements in which the stories told are never completed but are always open to reflection, capable of pushing ever further the boundaries of our collective imagination and struggles against injustice, wherever they might be. Only then will the stories that now cripple our imaginations, politics, and democracy be challenged and possibly overcome.

ONE

AMERICA'S DISIMAGINATION MACHINE

People who remember court madness through pain, the pain of the perpetually recurring death of their innocence; people who forget court another kind of madness, the madness of the denial of pain and the hatred of innocence.

—James Baldwin

America—a country in which forms of historical, political, and moral forgetting are not only willfully practiced, but celebrated—has become amnesiac. The United States has degenerated into a social order that views critical thought as both a liability and a threat. Not only is this obvious in the proliferation of a vapid culture of celebrity, but it is also present in the prevailing discourses and policies of a range of politicians and anti-public intellectuals who believe that the legacy of the Enlightenment needs to be reversed. Politicians such as Michelle Bachmann, Rick Santorum, and Newt Gingrich along with talking heads such as Bill O'Reilly, Glenn Beck, and Anne Coulter are not the problem. They are merely symptomatic of a much more disturbing assault on critical thought, if not rational thinking itself. The notion that education is central to producing a critically literate citizenry, which is indispensable to a democracy, is viewed in some conservative quarters as dangerous, if not treasonous. Under a neoliberal regime, the language of authority, power, and command is divorced from ethics, social responsibility, critical analysis, and social costs.

Today's anti-public intellectuals are part of a disimagination machine that consolidates the power of the rich and supports the interconnected grid of military, surveillance, corporate, and academic structures by presenting the ideologies, institutions, and relations of the powerful as both commonsense and natural.[1] For instance, the historical legacies of resistance to racism, militarism, privatization, and panoptical surveillance have long been forgotten in the current assumption that Americans now live in a democratic, post-racial society.[2] The cheerleaders for neoliberalism work hard to normalize dominant institutions and relations of power through a vocabulary and public pedagogy that create market-driven subjects, modes of consciousness, and ways of understanding the world that promote accommodation, quietism, and passivity. As social protections and other foundations provided by the social contract come under attack and disappear, Americans are increasingly losing their capacity for connection, community, and a sense of civic engagement.

The Rise of the "Disimagination Machine"

Adapting Georges Didi-Huberman's term "disimagination machine," I argue that a politics of disimagination has emerged, in which stories, images, institutions, discourses, and other modes of representation are undermining our capacity to bear witness to a different and critical sense of remembering, agency, ethics, and collective resistance.[3] The "disimagination machine" is both a set of cultural apparatuses—extending from schools and mainstream media to the new sites of screen culture—and a public pedagogy that functions primarily to short-circuit the ability of individuals to think critically, imagine the unimaginable, and engage in thoughtful and critical dialogue, or, put simply, to become critically engaged citizens of the world.

Examples of the "disimagination machine" abound. A few will suffice. For instance, the Texas State Board of Education and other conservative boards of education throughout the United States are rewriting American textbooks to promote and impose on America's public school students what Katherine Stewart calls "a Christian nationalist version of U.S. history" in which Jesus is implored to "invade" public schools.[4] In this version of history, the terms "human trafficking" and "slavery" are removed from textbooks and replaced with "Atlantic triangular trade;" Earth is merely 6,000 years old; and the Enlightenment is the enemy of education. Historical figures such as Thomas Jefferson, Thomas Paine, and Benjamin Franklin are now deemed to have suspect religious views and "are ruthlessly demoted or purged altogether from the study program."[5] Currently, 46 percent of the American population believes in the creationist view of evolution and increasingly rejects scientific evidence, research, and rationality as either "academic" or irreligious.[6]

The rise of the Tea Party and the renewal of culture

wars have resulted in a Republican Party that is now considered the righteous party of anti-science.[7] Similarly, right-wing politicians, media, talk show hosts, and other pundits loudly and widely spread the message that a culture of questioning is antithetical to the American way of life. Moreover, this message is also promoted by conservative groups such as the American Legislative Exchange Council, which "hit the ground running in 2013, pushing 'model bills' mandating the teaching of climate-change denial in public school systems."[8] Efforts to discredit climate change science are also promoted by powerful conservative groups such as the Heartland Institute. Ignorance is never too far from repression, as was demonstrated in Arizona when Representative Bob Thorpe, a Republican freshman Tea Party member, introduced a new bill requiring students to take a patriotic loyalty oath in order to receive a graduation diploma.[9]

The "disimagination machine"—though not entirely new to American culture—is more powerful than ever. Conservative think tanks provide ample funds for training and promoting anti-public pseudo-intellectuals and religious fundamentalists, while simultaneously offering policy statements and talking points to conservative media such as Fox News, Christian news networks, right-wing talk radio, and partisan social media and blogs. This ever-growing information-illiteracy bubble has become a powerful form of public pedagogy in the larger culture and is responsible not only for normalizing the war on science, reason, and critical thought, but also the war on women's reproductive rights, communities of color, low-income families, immigrants, unions, public schools, and any other group or institution that challenges the anti-intellectual, antidemocratic world views of the new extremists. Liberal democrats, of course, contribute to this "disimagination machine" through educational policies that substitute forms of critical thinking and education for paralyzing pedagogies of memorization and rote learning tied to high-stakes testing in the service of creating a dumbed down and compliant work force. As the U.S. government retreats from its responsibility to foster the common good, it joins with corporate power to transform public schools into sites of containment and repression, while universities are "coming under pressure to turn themselves into training schools equipping young people with the skills required by the modern economy."[10] The hidden order of politics in this instance is that the United States has become an increasingly corporate space dominated not only by the script of cost-benefit analysis but also one in which creative powers of citizenship are being redefined as a narrow set of consumer choices.

What further keeps the American public in a state of intellectual servitude and fuels the hysteria of Judeo-Christian nationalism is the perception of being constantly under threat—a thinly veiled justification for ramping up state and corporate surveillance while extending the tentacles of the national security state.[11] Through political messages filtered and spectacularized by the mass media, Americans have been increasingly encircled by a culture of fear and what Brad Evans has called "insecurity by design."[12] Americans are urged to adjust to survival mode, be resilient, and bear the weight of the times by themselves—all of which is code for a process of depoliticization.[13] The catastrophes and social problems produced by the financial elite and mega-corporations now become the fodder of an individualized politics, a space of risk in which one can exhibit fortitude and a show of hyper-masculine toughness. Or vulnerability is touted as a matter of common sense so as to mask the social, political, and economic forces that produce it, thus transforming it into an ideology whose purpose is to conceal power and encourage individuals to flee from any sense of social and political engagement. As Robin D. G. Kelley argues, "focusing on the personal obscures what is really at stake: ideas, ideology, the nature of change, the evisceration of our critical faculties under an appeal to neoliberal commonsense."[14]

In this instance, the call to revel in risk and vulnerability as a site of identity formation and ontological condition makes invisible the oppressive workings of power. But it does more—it undermines any viable faith in the future and reduces progress to a script that furthers the neoliberal goals of austerity, privatization, and the accumulation of capital in the hands of the ruling and corporate elite. Meaningful social solidarities are torn apart and deterred, furthering a retreat into orbits of the private and undermining those spaces that nurture non-commodified knowledge, public values, critical exchange, and civic literacy. The pedagogy of authoritarianism is alive and well in the United States, and its repression of public memory takes place not only through the screen culture and institutional apparatuses of conformity, but also through a climate of fear and the ominous presence of a carceral state that imprisons more people than any other country in the world.[15]

The stalwart enemies of manufactured fear and militant punitiveness are critical thought and the willingness to question authority—as is abundantly evident, for example, in the case of Edward Snowden and those who champion him. What many commentators have missed in regard to Snowden is that his actions have gone beyond revealing merely how intrusive the U.S. government has become and have demonstrated how willing the state is to engage in vast crimes against the American public in the service of repressing dissent and a culture of questioning. Snowden's real "crime" was that he demonstrated how knowledge can be used to empower the population to think and act as critically engaged communities fully capable of holding their government accountable. Snowden's exposure of the massive reach of the surveillance state with its biosensors, scanners, face-recognition technologies, miniature drones, high-speed computers, massive data-mining capabilities, and other stealth technologies made visible "the stark realities of disappearing privacy and diminishing liberties."[16] Making the workings of oppressive power visible has its costs, and Snowden has become a flashpoint revealing the willingness of the state to repress dissent regardless of how egregious such a practice might be.

Since the late 1970s, there has been an intensification in the United States, Canada, and Europe of neoliberal modes of governance, ideology, and policies—a historical period in which the foundations for democratic public spheres have been dismantled.[17] Schools, libraries, the airwaves, public parks and plazas, and other manifestations of the public sphere have been under siege, viewed as disadvantageous to a market-driven society that considers noncommercial imagination, critical thought, dialogue, and civic engagement a threat to its hierarchy of authoritarian operating systems, ideologies, and structures of power, domination, and control. The 1970s marked the beginning of a historical era in which the discourses of democracy, public values, and the common good came crashing to the ground. First Margaret Thatcher in Britain and then Ronald Reagan in the United States—both hard-line advocates of market fundamentalism—announced that there was no such thing as society and that government was the problem, not the solution. Democracy and the political process were all but sacrificed to the power of corporations and the emerging financial service industries, just as hope was appropriated as an advertisement for a whitewashed world in which the function of culture to counter oppressive social practices was greatly diminished.[18] Large social movements fragmented into isolated pockets of resistance mostly organized around a form of identity politics that largely ignored a much-needed conversation about the attack on the social and the broader issues affecting society, such as increasingly harmful disparities in wealth, power, and income. Tony Judt argues this point persuasively in his insistence that politics

> devolved into an aggregation of individual claims upon society and the state. "Identity" began to

colonize public discourse: private identity, sexual identity, cultural identity. From here it was but a short step to the fragmentation of radical politics, its metamorphosis into multiculturalism. . . . However legitimate the claims of individuals and the importance of their rights, emphasizing these carries an unavoidable cost: the decline of a shared sense of purpose. Once upon a time one looked to society—or class, or community—for one's normative vocabulary: what was good for everyone was by definition good for anyone. But the converse does not hold. What is good for one person may or may not be of value or interest to another. Conservative philosophers of an earlier age understood this well, which was why they resorted to *religious* language and imagery to justify traditional authority and its claims upon each individual.[19]

As forms of state sovereignty gave way to market-centered private modes of political control, the United States morphed into an increasingly authoritarian space in which young people became the most visible symbol of the collateral damage that resulted from the emergence, especially after 9/11, of a new kind of domestic terrorism. If the enemy abroad was defined as the Islamic other, young people increasingly obtained the status of the enemy at home, especially youthful protesters and young people of color. Neoliberalism's war on youth is significant as both a war on the future and on democracy itself. Youth are no longer the place where society reveals its dreams. Instead, youth are becoming the site of society's nightmares. Within neoliberal narratives, youth are defined opportunistically in terms of contradictory symbols, whether as a consumer market, a drain on the economy, or as an intransigent menace.[20]

Young people increasingly have become subject to an oppressive disciplinary system that teaches them to understand citizenship through the pecuniary practices of the market and to follow orders and toe the line in the face of authority, no matter how counterintuitive, unpleasant, or oppressive doing so may be. They are caught in a society in which almost every aspect of their lives is shaped by the dual forces of the market and a growing police state. The message is clear: get in on buying/selling or be ignored or punished. Mostly out of step, young people, especially people of color and low-income whites, are inscribed within a machinery of dead knowledge, social relations, and values in which there is an attempt to render them voiceless and invisible. Often relegated to sites of terminal exclusion, many young people are forced to negotiate their fates alone, bearing full responsibility for a society that forces them to bear the weight of problems that are not of their own making and for which they bear no personal blame. For example, what prospects are waiting for teenagers who age out of the foster care system at eighteen years old and go out into our minimum-wage society on their own? What future do they have? For many, the answer is military recruitment or prison. What is particularly new is the way in which young people have been increasingly denied a significant place in an already weakened social contract and the degree to which they are absent from how many countries' leaders now envision the future.[21]

How young people are represented betrays a great deal about the economic, social, cultural, and political constitution of American society and its growing disinvestment in young people, the social state, and democracy itself.[22] The structures of neoliberal violence have diminished the vocabulary of democracy, and one consequence is that subjectivity and education are no longer the lifelines of critical forms of individual and social agency. This is most evident in the attack on public schools in the United States, an attack that is as vicious as it is authoritarian. The war on schools by billionaires such as Bill Gates (Microsoft) and the Walton family (Walmart), among others, is attempting to corporatize classroom teaching by draining pedagogy of any of its critical functions while emphasizing "teaching to the test." Similarly, schools are being reorganized so as to eliminate the influence of unions and the power of teachers. As Michael Yates points out, they have begun "to resemble assembly lines, with students as outputs and teachers as assembly-line-like mechanisms who do not think or instill in their students the capacity to conceptualize critically and become active participants in a democratic society."[23] Such schools have become punishing factories waging a war on the radical imagination and undermining those rationalities where desire is constructed and behavior specified that embraces civic courage and the common good.

The promises of modernity regarding progress, freedom, and hope as part of the project of extending and deepening the ideals of democracy have not been eliminated; they have been reconfigured, stripped of their emancipatory potential and relegated to the logic of a savage market instrumentality. Modernity has reneged on its promise to young people to provide them with social mobility, economic well-being, and collective security. Long-term planning and the institutional structures that support it are now fully subservient to the financial imperatives of privatization, deregulation, commodification, flexibility, and short-term profits. Social bonds have fragmented as a result of the attack on the welfare state and the collapse of social protections. Moreover, all possible answers to socially produced problems are now limited to the mantra of individual, market-based solutions.[24] It gets worse. Increasingly, those individuals and groups who question the savage logic of the free market or are unable to function within it as atomized employees/consumers are viewed contemptuously as either traitors or moochers and are rendered disposable by corporate and government elites.[25]

Public problems now collapse into the limited and depoliticized register of private issues. Individual self-interest now trumps any consideration of the good society just as all problems are ultimately laid at the door of the solitary individual whose fate is shaped by forces far beyond his or her personal control. Under neoliberalism, everyone has to negotiate their fate alone, bearing full responsibility for problems that are often not of their own doing. The implications politically, economically, and socially for young people are disastrous and are contributing to the emergence of a generation that will populate a space of social abandonment and terminal exclusion. Job insecurity, debt servitude, impoverishment, enlistment to war zones, incarceration, and a growing network of real and symbolic violence have dismissed too many young people to a future that portends zero opportunities and zero hope. This is a generation that has become a primary target for disposability through prison or war, consignment to debt, and new levels of surveillance and consumer control.

The severity and consequences of this shift for youth are evident in the fact that this will be the first generation in which the "plight of the outcast may stretch to embrace a whole generation."[26] Zygmunt Bauman argues that today's youth have been "cast in a condition of liminal drift, with no way of knowing whether it is transitory or permanent."[27] That is, the generation of youth in the early twenty-first century has no way of grasping if it will ever "be free from the gnawing sense of the transience, indefiniteness, and provisional nature of any settlement."[28] Neoliberal violence—originating in part from a massive accumulation of wealth by the elite 1 percent of society, growing inequality, the reign of the financial service industries, the closing down of educational opportunities, and the stripping of social protections from those marginalized by race and class—has produced an entire generation without jobs, an independent life, and even the most minimal social benefits.

Youth no longer inhabit the privileged space, however compromised, that was offered to previous generations.

They now move listlessly through a neoliberal notion of temporality as dead time, devoid of faith in progress and entranced by a belief in those apocalyptic narratives in which the future appears indeterminate, bleak, and insecure. Progressive visions pale and recede next to the normalization of wealth-driven policies that wipe out pensions, punish unions, demonize public servants, raise college tuition, and produce a harsh world of joblessness—all the while giving billions of dollars and "huge bonuses, instead of prison sentences . . . to those bankers and investment brokers who were responsible for the 2008 meltdown of the economy and the loss of homes for millions of Americans."[29] Students, in particular, now find themselves in a world in which heightened expectations have been replaced by dashed hopes. The promises of higher education and previously enviable credentials have turned into their opposite: "For the first time in living memory, the whole class of graduates faces a future of crushing debt, and a high probability, almost the certainty, of ad hoc, temporary, insecure and part-time work and unpaid 'trainee' pseudo-jobs deceitfully rebranded as 'practices'—all considerably below the skills they have acquired and eons below the level of their expectations."[30]

What has changed for an entire generation of young people includes not only neoliberal society's disinvestment in youth and the lasting fate of downward mobility, but also the fact that youth live in a commercially saturated and commodified environment that is unlike anything previously imposed. Nothing has prepared this generation for the inhospitable and savage new world of commodifica-

tion, privatization, joblessness, frustrated hopes, and still-
born projects.[31] Advertising provides the primary imagery
for their dreams, relations to others, identities, and sense
of agency. There appears to be no space outside the pan-
opticon of commercial debasement and casino capitalism.
The present generation has been born into a throwaway
world of consumption and control in which both goods
and people are increasingly viewed as entirely disposable.
Young people now reside in a world in which there remain
few public spheres or social spaces beyond the controlling
influence of the market, the warfare state, debtfare, and
sprawling tentacles of the NSA and its national surveillance
apparatus.

The structures of neoliberal modernity do more than
disinvest from young people: they also transform the protected space of childhood into a zone of disciplinary exclusion and cruelty, especially for those families who are
marginalized by race, class, and residency status and who
are forced to occupy a social landscape in which they are
increasingly disparaged as flawed consumers or pathologized others. With no adequate role to play as owners and
consumers, many youth are now considered disposable,
forced to inhabit "zones of social abandonment" extending
from homeless shelters and impoverished schools to bulg-
ing detention centers and prisons.[32] In the midst of the rise
of the punishing state, the circuits of state repression, surveillance, and disposability "link the fate of blacks, Latinos,
Native Americans, poor whites, and Asian Americans" who
are caught in a governing-through-crime youth complex

that essentially serves as a default solution to major social problems.[33] As Michael Hardt and Antonio Negri point out, young people live in a society in which every institution becomes an "inspection regime"—recording, watching, gathering information and storing data.[34] Complementing these regimes is the shadow of the prison which is no longer separated from society as an institution of total surveillance. Instead, "total surveillance is increasingly the general condition of society as a whole. "The prison," Michel Foucault notes, "begins well before its doors. It begins as soon as you leave your house—and even before."[35]

Everyone Is Now a Potential Terrorist

Today young people all over the world are building movements against a variety of grievances ranging from economic injustice and massive inequality to drastic cuts in education and public services. These social networks have and currently are being met with state-sanctioned violence and an almost pathological refusal to respond to the articulation of social needs and demands. In the United States, the state monopoly on the use of violence has intensified since the 1980s, and in the process has been increasingly directed against youth, low-income populations, communities of color, people with disputed residency status, and women. As the welfare state is hollowed out, a culture of compassion is replaced by a culture of violence and cruelty. Collective insurance policies and social protections have given way to the forces of corporate predation, the transformation of the welfare state into punitive workfare programs, the privatization of public goods, and an appeal to individual competition and ambition as a substitute for civic agency and community engagement.

Under the notion that unregulated market-driven values and relations should shape every domain of human life, the business model of governance has eviscerated any viable notion of social responsibility while furthering the criminalization of social problems and cutbacks in basic social services, especially for young people, the elderly, people of color, and the impoverished.[36] At this historical juncture there is a merging of violence and governance along with the systemic disinvestment in and breakdown of institutions and public spheres that have provided the minimal conditions for democracy. This becomes obvious in the emergence of a surveillance state in which social media not only become new platforms for the invasion of privacy but further legitimate a culture in which monitoring functions are viewed as both necessary and benign. Meanwhile, the state-sponsored society of hyper-fear increasingly regards each and every person as a potential terrorist suspect.

The war on terrorism has increasingly morphed into a war on dissent. As Kate Epstein argues, one "very real purpose of the surveillance programs—and perhaps the entire war on terror—is to target and repress political dissent. 'Terrorism' is the new 'Communism,' and the war on terror and all its shiny new surveillance technology is the new Cold War and McCarthyism."[37] Everyone, especially people in communities of color, now adjusts to a panoptical existence in which "living under constant surveillance means living as criminals."[38] As young people make diverse claims on the promise of a renewed democracy, articulating what a fair and just world might be, they are increasingly met with forms of physical, ideological, and structural violence. Abandoned by the existing political system, young people in Oakland, New York City, Montreal, and numerous other cities throughout the globe have placed their bodies on the line, protesting peacefully while trying to develop new organizations for democracy, to imagine long-term institutions, and to support notions of "community that manifest the values of equality and mutual respect that they see missing in a world that is structured by neoliberal principles."[39] In Quebec, despite police violence and threats, thousands of students demonstrated for months against a former right-wing government that wanted to raise tuition and cut social protections. Such demonstrations against the language and politics of austerity have taken place in a variety of countries throughout the world and embrace a new understanding of the commons as a shared space of participatory knowledge, enrichment, debate, and exchange.

These movements are thinking beyond a financialized notion of exchange based exclusively on notions of buying and selling. They are not simply about addressing current injustices and reclaiming space, but also about reawakening the social imagination, acting on new ideas, advancing new conversations, and embodying a new political language. Rejecting the corporate line that democracy and markets are the same, young people are calling for an end to the normalization of chronic impoverishment, accelerating economic inequality, the suppression of dissent, and the permanent war state. Today's movement-building youth refuse to be acknowledged exclusively as consumers or to accept that the only interests that matter are fiscal. These creative young people and the movements they are advancing are raising a diverse range of voices in opposition to market-driven values and practices that aim at both limiting agency to civic community and undermining those public spheres that create networks of solidarity and reinforce a commitment to the common good.

Resistance and the Politics of the Historical Conjuncture

Marginalized youth, workers, artists, and others are raising serious questions about the violence of inequality and the authoritarian hierarchies that legitimate it. They are calling for a redistribution of wealth and power—not within the old system but in a new one in which democracy becomes more than a slogan or a legitimation for authoritarianism and state violence. As Angela Y. Davis and Stanley Aronowitz, among others, have argued, the fight for education and justice is inseparable from the struggle for economic equality, human dignity, and security, and the challenge of developing American institutions along genuinely democratic lines. Today, there is a new focus on public values, the need for broad-based movements, and imagining viable systems for securing democracy, social justice, and ecological sustainability. And while the visibility of youth protests have waned, many young people are working locally to forge a deeper notion of justice, one in which appeals to justice are matched by effort to change the dominant ideologies and structural relations that inform everyday life.

All of these issues are important, but what must be addressed in the most immediate sense is the threat posed by the emerging surveillance state in the United States. Beyond targeting the activists of all ages who are rising up in a number of American cities, the militarization of society poses a clear threat to democracy itself. This threat is being exacerbated as a result of the merging of a warlike mentality and neoliberal modes of discipline and education in which it becomes difficult to reclaim the language of conscience, social responsibility, and civic engagement.[40] Everywhere we look we see the encroaching shadow of the national surveillance state. The government now requisitions personal telephone records and sifts through private emails. It labels whistleblowers, such as Edward Snowden, traitors, even though they have exposed the corruption and lawlessness practiced on an ongoing basis by elite authorities who operate above and beyond the laws to which the rest of the population are subjected. While state authorities spy on the general population and bankers commit acts of economic mass destruction with virtual impunity, ordinary Americans go to jail by the thousands simply for protesting. For example, in a 24-month period, more than 7,000 people went to jail for participating in protests associated with the Occupy movement.[41] The U.S currently imprisons over 2.3 million human beings while "6 million people at any one time [are] under carceral supervision—more than were in Stalin's Gulag."[42]

While little national attention is given to the thousands of arrests and acts of violence that were waged against the Occupy movement and other protesters, it is important to situate such state aggression within a broader set of categories that not only enables a better understanding of the underlying social, economic, and political forces at work in such assaults, but also allows us to reflect critically on the distinctiveness of the current historical period in which such repression of democracy is taking place. For example, it is difficult to address state-sponsored violence against free speech and protest without analyzing the devolution of the social state and the corresponding rise of the warfare and punishing state.

Stuart Hall's reworking of Gramsci's notion of conjuncture is important here because it provides both a conceptual opening into the forces shaping a particular historical moment and a framework for merging theory and strategy.[43] Conjuncture in this case refers to a period in which different elements of society come together to produce a unique fusion of the economic, social, political, ideological, and cultural in a relative settlement that becomes hegemonic in defining reality. That fusion is today marked by a neoliberal conjuncture. In this particular historical moment, the notion of conjuncture helps us to address theoretically how state surveillance and repression of free speech and widespread nonviolent protests are largely related to a historically specific neoliberal project that advances vast inequalities in income and wealth, creates the student loan debt bomb, eliminates much-needed social programs, eviscerates the social wage, and privileges profit over people. Youth today live in a period of history marked by an "epochal crisis" in which they are largely considered disposable, relegated to the savage dictates of a survival-of-the-fittest society in which they are now considered on their own and governed by a generalized fear of being unemployed or not being able to survive.[44]

Within the United States especially, the often violent response to nonviolent forms of social protest must also be analyzed within the framework of a mammoth military-industrial state and its commitment to war and the militarization of the entire society.[45] The merging of the military-industrial complex, the surveillance state, and unbridled corporate power points to the need for strategies that address what is specific about the current neoliberal warfare state and how different interests, modes of power, social relations, public pedagogies, and economic configurations come together to shape its politics. Thinking in terms of such a conjuncture is invaluable politically in that it provides a theoretical opening for making the practices of the warfare state and the neoliberal revolution visible in order "to give the resistance to its onward march content, focus, and a cutting edge."[46] It also points to the conceptual power of making clear that history remains an open horizon that cannot be dismissed through appeals to the end of history or end of ideology.[47] It is precisely through the indeterminate nature of history that resistance becomes possible and politics refuses any guarantees and remains open.

I want to argue that the current historical moment or what Stuart Hall called the "long march of the Neoliberal Revolution" is best understood in terms of the growing forms of violence that it deploys and reinforces.[48] Such anti-democratic pressures and their relationship to protests in the United States and abroad are evident in the crisis that has emerged through the integration of governance and violence, the growth of the punishing state, and the persistent development of what has been described by Alex Honneth as "a failed sociality."[49] The United States has become addicted to violence, and this dependency is *fueled* increasingly by its willingness to wage war at home and abroad.

War in this instance is not merely the outgrowth of policies designed to protect the security and well-being of the United States. It is also, as C. Wright Mills pointed out, part of a "military metaphysics"—a complex of forces that includes corporations, defense industries, politicians, financial institutions, and universities.[50] War provides jobs, profits, political payoffs, research funds, and forms of political and economic power that reach into every aspect of society. Waging war is also one of the nation's most honored virtues, and its militaristic values now bear down on almost every aspect of American life.[51] As modern society is increasingly defined by the realities of permanent war, a carceral state, and a national surveillance infrastructure, the social stature of the military and soldiers has risen.[52] As Michael Hardt and Tony Negri point out: "In the United States, rising esteem for the military in uniform corresponds to the growing militarization of the society as a whole. All of this despite repeated revelations of the illegality and immorality of the military's own incarceration systems, from Guantánamo to Abu Ghraib, whose systematic practices border on if not actually constitute torture."⁵³ The state of exception in the United States, in particular, has become permanent and promises no end. War has become a mode of sovereignty and rule, eroding the distinctions between war and peace, defense and provocation. Increasingly fed by a coordinated moral and political hysteria, warlike values produce and endorse shared fears as the primary register of social relations.

The war on terror, rebranded under Obama as the "Overseas Contingency Operation," has morphed into a war on democracy. Everyone is now considered a potential terrorist, providing a rationale for both the government and private corporations to spy on anybody, regardless of whether they have yet to be suspected of a crime. Surveillance is supplemented by increasingly militarized police forces that now receive intelligence, weapons, and training from federal authorities like the Department of Homeland Security. Military technologies such as drones, SWAT vehicles, and machine-gun-equipped armored trucks once used exclusively in combat zones such as Iraq and Afghanistan are now being supplied to local police departments across the nation, and not surprisingly "the increase in such weapons is matched by training local police in war zone tactics and strategies."⁵⁴

The domestic war against "terrorists" [increasingly a code for those who dare to protest] provides new opportunities for major defense contractors and corporations who "are becoming more a part of our domestic lives."⁵⁵ As Glenn Greenwald points out, "Arming domestic police forces with para-military weaponry will ensure their systematic use even in the absence of a terrorist attack on U.S. soil; they will simply find other, increasingly permissive uses for those weapons."[56]

Of course, the new domestic paramilitary forces will also undermine free speech and dissent with the threat of force while simultaneously threatening core civil liberties, human rights, and civic responsibilities. Given that "by age 23, almost a third of Americans are arrested for a crime," it becomes clear that in the new militarized state young people, especially those in communities of color, are viewed as predators and treated as either a threat to corporate governance or a disposable population.[57] This siege mentality will only be reinforced by the collaboration of the state with private intelligence and surveillance agencies; the violence such an alliance produces will increase, as will the growth of a punishment state that acts with impunity. Scholars like Michelle Alexander demonstrate that this contemporary violence is in many ways an extension of the state's application of Jim Crow laws, which themselves extended from the generations of domestic terror that white enslavers institutionalized to control people they had bought, bred, and sold for profit.[58]

Yet there is more at work here than the prevalence of armed knowledge and a militarized discourse: there is also the emergence of a militarized society that now organizes itself "for the production of violence."[59] America has become a society in which "the range of acceptable opinion inevitably shrinks."[60] War has become normalized and no longer needs to be declared. The targets of war increasingly expand from communities of color and immigrants to youth, low-income women, and unions. War is no longer aimed at restoring peace but sacrificing it, along with any hope for a different future. The endless updating of a machinery of warfare and death has not just become permanent, it has become a booming growth industry. The normalization of permanent war does more than promote a set of unifying symbols that embrace a survival-of-the-fittest ethic, favoring conformity over dissent, the strong over the weak, and fear over responsibility. It also gives rise to what David Graeber has called a "language of command" in which violence becomes the most important element of power and a mediating force in shaping most, if not all, social relationships.[61]

Permanent War and the Public Pedagogy of Acceptable Ambient Violence

A permanent war state inevitably relies on modes of public pedagogy that influence willing subjects to abide by its values, ideology, and narratives of fear and violence. Such legitimation in the United States today is largely provided through a market-driven system addicted to the production of consumerism, militarism, and organized violence that circulates through various registers of commercial culture extending from television shows and Hollywood movies to violent video games and music concerts sponsored by the Pentagon. The market-driven spectacle of war demands a culture of compliance: silenced intellectuals and a fully entertained population distracted from the living nightmare of correctable injustices all around them. There is also a need for subjects who can be shaped to derive pleasure in the commodification of violence and a culture of cruelty. Under neoliberalism, culture appears to have largely abandoned its role as a site of critique. Very little appears to escape the infantilizing influence and moral vacuity of those who run the market. Film, television, video games, children's toys, cartoons, and even high fashion are all shaped to normalize a society centered on war and violence. For instance, in 2013, following disclosure of NSA and PRISM spying revelations, the *New York Times* ran a story on a new line of fashion with the byline: "Stealth Wear Aims to Make a Tech Statement."[62]

As the pleasure principle becomes less constrained by a moral compass based on a respect for others, it is increasingly shaped by the need for intense excitement and a never-ending flood of heightened sensations. Advanced by commercialized notions of aggression and cruelty, a culture of violence has become commonplace in a social order in which pain, humiliation, and abuse are condensed into digestible spectacles endlessly circulated through new and old forms of media and entertainment. But the ideology and the economy of pleasure it justifies are also present in the material relations of power that have intensified since the Reagan presidency, when a shift in government policies first took place and set the stage for the contemporary reemergence of unchecked torture and state violence under the Bush-Cheney regime. Conservative and liberal politicians alike now spend millions waging wars around the globe, funding the largest military state in the world, providing huge tax benefits to the ultra-rich and major corporations, and all the while draining public coffers, increasing the scale of human poverty and misery, and eliminating all viable public spheres—whether they be the social state, public schools, public transportation, or any other aspect of a democratic culture that addresses the needs of the common good.

State violence—particularly the use of torture, abductions, and targeted assassinations—is now justified as part of a state of exception in which a "political culture of hyper-punitiveness" has become normalized.[63] Revealing itself in a blatant display of unbridled arrogance and power, it appears unchecked by any sense of conscience or morality. How else to explain right-wing billionaire Charles Koch insisting that the best way to help the poor is to get rid of the minimum wage? In response, journalist Rod Bastanmehr pointed out that "Koch didn't acknowledge the growing gap between the haves and the have-nots, but he did make sure to show off his fun new roll of $100-bill toilet paper, which was a real treat for folks everywhere."[64] It gets worse. Ray Canterbury, a Republican member of the West Virginia House of Delegates, insisted that "students could be forced into labor in exchange for food."[65] In other words, students could clean toilets, do janitorial work, or other menial chores in order to pay for their free school breakfast and lunch programs. In Maine, Republican Representative Bruce Bickford has argued that the state should do away with child labor laws. His rationale speaks for itself. He writes: "Kids have parents. Let the parents be responsible for the kids. It's not up to the government to regulate everybody's life and lifestyle. Take the government away. Let the parents take care of their kids."[66]

This is a version of Social Darwinism on steroids, a tribute to Ayn Rand that would make even her blush.

Public values are not only under attack in the United States and elsewhere they appear to have become irrelevant. Those spaces that once enabled an experience of the common good are now disdained by right-wing and liberal politicians, anti-public intellectuals, and an army of media pundits. State violence operating under the guise of increasing personal safety and security, while parading as a bulwark of democracy, actually does the opposite and cancels out democracy "as the incommensurable sharing of existence that makes the political possible."[67] Symptoms of ethical, political, and economic impoverishment are all around us. One recent example can be found in the farm bill passed by Republicans, which provides $195 billion in subsidies for agribusiness, while slashing roughly $8 billion from the Supplemental Nutrition Assistance Program (SNAP). SNAP provides food stamps for people living below the poverty line. Not only are millions of food stamp beneficiaries still at risk for malnourishment and starvation, it is estimated that benefits would be entirely eliminated for nearly two million Americans, many of them children. Katrina vanden Heuvel writes in the *Washington Post* that it is hard to believe that any party would want to publicize such cruel practices. She states:

> In this time of mass unemployment, 47 million Americans rely on food stamps. Nearly one-half are children under 18; nearly 10 percent are impov-

erished seniors. The recipients are largely white,
female and young. The Republican caucus has de-
cided to drop them from the bill as "extraneous,"
without having separate legislation to sustain them.
Who would want to advertise these cruel values?[68]

Neoliberal policies have produced proliferating zones
of precarity and exclusion that are enveloping more and
more individuals and groups who lack jobs, need social assistance and health care, or are homeless. According to the
apostles of modern-day capitalism, providing "nutritional
aid to millions of pregnant mothers, infants, and children
. . . feeding poor children, and giving them adequate health
care" is a bad expenditure because it creates "a culture of
dependency—and that culture of dependency, not runaway
bankers, somehow caused our economic crisis."[69] What is
left out of the spurious and cruel assertion that social provisions create a culture of dependency, especially with respect
to the food stamp program, is that "six million Americans
receiving food stamps report they have no other income.
[Many describe] themselves as unemployed and receiving
no cash aid—no welfare, no unemployment insurance, and
no pensions, child support or disability pay. . . . About one
in 50 Americans now lives in a household with a reported
income that consists of nothing but a food-stamp card."[70]
Needless to say, there is more to the culture of cruelty than
ethically challenged policies that benefit the rich and punish
the poor, particularly children. There is also the emergence
of a carceral state that operates a governing-through-crime

youth complex and a school-to-prison pipeline that essentially functions as a new extension of Jim Crow.[71]

The strengthening of the school-to-prison pipeline—seen in the increased acceptance of criminalizing the behavior of young people in public schools—is a grotesque symptom of the way in which violence has saturated everyday life. Behaviors that were normally handled by teachers, guidance counselors, and school administrators are now dealt with by the police and the criminal justice system. Under such circumstances, not only do schools resemble the culture of prisons, but young children are being arrested and subjected to court appearances for behaviors that can only be termed as trivial. How else to explain the case of a diabetic student who, because she fell asleep in study hall, was arrested and beaten by the police or the arrest of a seven-year-old boy who, because of a fight he got into with another boy in the schoolyard, was put in handcuffs and held in custody for ten hours in a Bronx police station?[72] In Texas, students who miss school are not sent to the principal's office or assigned detention. Instead, they are fined and in too many cases actually jailed.[73] It is hard to imagine, but in a Maryland school, a thirteen-year-old girl was arrested for refusing to say the pledge of allegiance.[74] In these examples, we see more at work than stupidity and a flight from responsibility on the part of educators, parents, and politicians who maintain these laws. We see actions motivated by an underlying belief and growing sentiment that young people constitute a threat to adults and that the only way to deal with them is to subject them to mind-crushing punishment.

The consequences have been disastrous for many young people. Even more disturbing is how the legacy of slavery informs these practices, given that "arrests and police interactions . . . disproportionately affect low-income schools with large African-American and Latino populations."[75] Instead of schools being a pipeline to opportunity, low-income white youth and children of color are being funneled directly from schools into prisons. Feeding the expanding prison-industrial complex, justified by the war on drugs, the United States is in the midst of a prison binge made obvious by the fact that "since 1970, the number of people behind bars . . . has increased 600 percent."[76] It is estimated that in some cities, such as Washington D.C., 75 percent of young black men can expect to serve time in prison. Michelle Alexander has pointed out that "one in three young African American men is currently under the control of the criminal justice system—in prison, in jail, on probation, or on parole—yet mass incarceration tends to be categorized as a criminal justice issue as opposed to a racial justice or civil rights issue (or crisis)."[77]

Young people of color in America have an ascribed identity that is a direct legacy of the society created by generations of white enslavers. Black men are particularly considered threatening, expendable, and part of a culture of criminality. They are deemed guilty of criminal behavior not because of the alleged crimes they might commit, but because a collective imagination paralyzed by the racism of a white supremacist culture that can only view them as a disturbing threat. Clearly, the real threat resides in a social order that hides behind the mutually informing and poisonous notions of colorblindness and a post-racial society, a convenient rhetorical obfuscation that allows white Americans to ignore the institutional and individual ideologies, practices, and policies that support toxic forms of racism and destroy any viable notions of justice and democracy. As the Trayvon Martin and Jordan Davis cases made clear, when young black men are not being arrested and channeled into the criminal justice system in record numbers, they are being targeted by vigilantes and private security forces and in some instances killed because they are black and assumed to be dangerous—or in Davis's case because he was playing loud rap music.[78] This medieval type of punishment inflicts pain on both the psyches and bodies of young people as part of a public spectacle of domination and subordination.

Anyone belonging to a population identified and treated as disposable faces an existence in which the ravages of segregation, racism, poverty, and dashed hopes are amplified by the forces of "privatization, financialization, militarization, and criminalization," fashioning a new architecture of punishment, massive human suffering, and authoritarianism.[79] Students being miseducated, criminalized, and arrested through a form of penal pedagogy in prison-type schools provide a grim reminder of the degree to which the ethos of containment and punishment now creeps into spheres of everyday life that were largely immune in the past from this type of state violence. This is not merely barbarism parading as reform—it is also a blatant indicator of the degree to which sadism and the infatuation with violence have become normalized in a society that seems to take delight in dehumanizing most of its population.

Widespread violence now functions as part of an anti-immune system that turns the economy of sadistic pleasure into the foundation for sapping democracy of any political substance and moral vitality. Democracy in the United States is increasingly battered by a collusion between financial elites and a surveillance state that de-prioritizes their "complex" crimes of economic mass destruction.[80] An American disimagination machine producing civic death and historical amnesia penetrates into all aspects of national life, suggesting that all who are marginalized by class, race, and ethnicity have been permanently abandoned. But historical and public memory are not merely on the side of those enforcing domination.

Anthropologist David Price asserts that historical memory can be a source of renewal within the "desert of organized forgetting" and suggests a rethinking of the role that artists, intellectuals, educators, youth, and other concerned citizens can play in fostering a "reawakening America's battered public memories."[81]Against the tyranny of forgetting, educators, young people, social activists, public intellectuals, workers and others can make visible and oppose the long legacy and current reality of state violence and the rise of the punishing state. Such a struggle suggests not only reclaiming, for instance, education as a public good but also reforming the criminal justice system and removing police from schools. In addition, there is a need to employ public memory, critical theory, and other intellectual archives and

resources to expose the crimes of those market-driven criminogenic regimes of power that now run the commanding
institutions of society and that have transformed the welfare
state into a warfare state.

The consolidation of capitalism, counterintelligence,
and the carceral state with their vast apparatuses of real and
symbolic violence must also be situated and understood as
part of a broader historical and political attack on public values, civic literacy, activism, and social justice. Crucial here is
the need to engage how such an attack is aided and abetted
by the emergence of a poisonous neoliberal public pedagogy
that depoliticizes as much as it entertains and corrupts. State
violence cannot be defined as simply a political issue. Also
operating in tandem with politics are pedagogical forces
that wage violence against the minds, desires, bodies, and
identities of young people as part of the reconfiguration of
the social state into the punishing state. At the heart of this
transformation is the emergence of a new form of corporate
sovereignty, a more intense form of state violence, a ruthless
survival-of-the-fittest ethic used to legitimate the concentrated power of the rich, and a concerted effort to punish
young people who are out of step with official lists, ideology,
values, and modes of social control.

Making young people bear the burden of a severe educational deficit has enormous currency in a society in which
existing relations of power are normalized. Under such
conditions, those who hold power accountable are viewed
as treasonous while critically engaged young people are denounced as un-American.[82] In any totalitarian society, dis-

sent is a threat, civic literacy is denounced, and those public spheres that produce engaged citizens are dismantled or impoverished through the substitution of genuine education with job training. Edward Snowden, for one, was denounced as being part of a generation that combined being educated with a distrust of authority. It is important to note that Snowden was labeled as a spy, not a whistle-blower—even though he exposed the reach of the spy services into the lives of most Americans. Of course, these antidemocratic tendencies represent more than a threat to young people: they also put in peril all of those communities, individuals, groups, public spheres, and institutions now considered disposable because they are at odds with a world run by bankers and the financial elite. Only a well-organized movement of young people, educators, workers, parents, religious groups, and other concerned citizens will be capable of changing the power relations and vast economic inequalities responsible for turning the United States into a country in which it is almost impossible to recognize the ideals of a real democracy.

Learning to Remember

The rise of America's disimagination machine and its current governing-through-punishment operating system suggest the need for a politics that not only negates the established order but imagines a new one, one informed by a radical vision in which the future does not imitate the present.[83] Learning to remember means merging a critique of the way things are with a sense of realistic hope or what I call educated hope, and transforming individual memories and struggles into collective narratives and larger social movements. The resistance that young people are mobilizing against oppressive societies all over the globe is being met with state-sponsored violence that is about more than militant police brutality. This is especially clear in the United States, where the shift from social welfare to a constant warfare state has replaced a culture of civic responsibility and democratic vision with one of cruelty, fear, and commodification. Until educators, artists, intellectuals, and various social movements address how the metaphysics of casino capitalism, war, and violence currently permeate American society (and societies in other parts of the world) along with the savage social costs it has enacted, the forms of social, political, and economic violence that ordinary people are protesting against, as well as the violence waged in response to their protests, will become impossible to recognize and counteract.

If acts of resistance are to matter, demonstrations and protests must give way to more sustainable organizations that develop alternative communities, autonomous forms of worker control, universal forms of health care, models of direct democracy, and emancipatory modes of education. Education must become central to any viable notion of politics willing to struggle for a life and future outside of predatory capitalism and the surveillance state that protects it. Teachers, young people, artists, and other cultural workers must come together to develop an educative and emancipatory politics in which people can address the historical, structural, and ideological conditions at the core of the violence being waged by the corporate and repressive state as well as begin to imagine a different collective future.

The issue of who gets to define the future not only rests on the questions of who controls global resources and who establishes the parameters of the social state. It also depends on who takes responsibility for creating a formative culture capable of producing democratically engaged and socially responsible citizens. This is much more than a rhetorical issue. Urgently required are new categories of community, identity, thought, and action that can form the basis for educating the public and generating broad-based structural changes. At stake here is the need for a language of both critique and possibility. Such a discourse will be utterly crucial for developing a politics that restores the promise of democracy and makes it a goal worth fighting for and winning.

TWO

THE NEW AUTHORITARIANISM

A society consisting of the sum of its vanity and greed is not a society at all but a state of war.

—Lewis Lapham

Ongoing debates in Washington and the mainstream media over austerity measures, the realities of a fiscal cliff, and the ever deepening national debt have produced what the late sociologist C. Wright Mills once called "a politics of organized irresponsibility"[1]—not least of all by obscuring the authoritarian pressures that are intensifying efforts to subvert American democracy. For Mills, authoritarian politics developed by making the operations of power invisible, while weaving a network of lies and deceptions in which isolated issues became disconnected from the broader relations and historical contexts that gave them meaning. Today these isolated issues have become flashpoints in a cultural and political discourse that conceals not merely the operations of power but also the resurgence of authoritarian ideologies, modes of social control, policies, and social formations that put any viable notion of democracy at risk.[2] Decontextualized ideas and issues coupled with an overflow of information produced by new electronic media make it more difficult to create coherent narratives that offer historical understanding, relational connections, and developmental sequences. The fragmentation of ideas and corresponding cascade of information reinforce new modes of depoliticization and authoritarianism.[3]

At the same time, important issues are buried in the fog of what Gerald Epstein has appropriately called *manufactured crises*. These crises are designed to stir popular sentiment but actually legitimize policies that benefit the wealthy and hurt working- and middle-class communities. For example, Epstein rightly argues that the debate about the fiscal cliff is

> a debacle on the part of the Obama administration and for progressives and for workers and for families. It's a real disaster . . . we shouldn't be having to sit here talking about this; we should be talking about what are going to do about the employment cliff or the climate change cliff. But instead we're talking about this fiscal cliff, which is a manufactured crisis.[4]

The fiscal cliff argument—rather than the so-called fiscal cliff itself—is possibly a real crisis in that it serves to divert attention away from pressing issues ranging from chronic mass unemployment and widespread impoverishment to unprosecuted crimes of economic mass destruction and the relationship between corporate predation and the housing crisis and the student debt bomb. And while neglecting the economic impacts on impoverished and middle-class families, this politics of distraction works assiduously to undermine any collective understanding of how economic, cultural, and social problems are interrelated ideologically and structurally as part of an assault by market fundamentalists on all aspects of public life that address and advance the common good.

In such a discourse of disconnection, the expanded reach of politics becomes fragmented. Private troubles are separated from public considerations, thereby narrowing our capacity to perceive the confluence of socio-economic-cultural interests and the prevailing issues of our particular political moment. For instance, the debate on gun control says little about the deep-rooted culture of symbolic and structural violence that nourishes America's infatuation with guns and its attraction to spectacles of violence. Similarly, the mainstream debate over taxing the rich refuses to address this issue through a broader analysis of a society that is structurally wedded to perpetrating massive inequities in wealth, health, nutrition, education, and mobility along with the considerable suffering and hardships entailed by such social disparities.

In this denuded version of politics, the relationships between personal troubles and larger social realities are covered over. Very little foundation remains on which we can build connections between facts and wider theoretical frameworks in order to strengthen the public's awareness of power and its operations. Under such circumstances, politics is stripped of its democratic elements. Informed modes of dissent are not only marginalized but also actively suppressed, as became obvious in 2011 with the federal surveillance of the Occupy movement and the police's ruthless suppression of student dissenters on campuses across the country.

Anesthetized Publics in an Authoritarian Age

What is missing in the recurring debates that dominate Washington politics is the recognition that the real issue at stake is neither the debt ceiling nor the state of the economy, but a powerful form of authoritarianism that poses a threat to the very idea of democracy and the institutions, public values, formative cultures, and public spheres that nourish it.[5] The United States nears a critical juncture in its history, one in which the rising forces of market extremism—left unchecked—will recalibrate modes of governance, ideology, and policy to provide fantastic wealth and legal immunity to an untouchable elite. The politics of disconnection is just one of a series of strategies designed to conceal this deeper order of authoritarian politics. In a society that revels in bouts of historical and social amnesia, it has become much easier for the language of politics and community to be appropriated and distorted so as to deplete words such as "democracy," "freedom," "justice," and the "social state" of any viable meaning. Arundhati Roy captures the antidemocratic nature of this process in the following insightful comment:

This theft of language, this technique of usurping

words and deploying them like weapons, of using them to mask intent and to mean exactly the opposite of what they have traditionally meant, has been one of the most brilliant strategic victories of the tsars of the new dispensation. It has allowed them to marginalize their detractors, deprive them of a language to voice their critique and dismiss them as being "anti-progress," "anti-development," "anti-reform," and of course "anti-national"—negativists of the worst sort. To reclaim these stolen words requires explanations that are too tedious for a world with a short attention span, and too expensive in an era when Free Speech has become unaffordable for the poor. This language heist may prove to be the keystone of our undoing.[6]

From the ailing rib of democracy there is emerging not only an aggressive political assault on democratic modes of governance, but also a form of linguistic and cultural authoritarianism that no longer needs to legitimate itself in an idea because it secures its foundational beliefs in a claim to normalcy.[7] The undoing of democracy to which Roy refers— and the dystopian society that is emerging in its place—can be observed in the current subordination of public values to commercial imperatives and an increasingly militarized carceral state. That is, Americans are now openly monitored and evaluated by an authoritarian system whose ideology, hierarchies, practices, and social formations cannot be questioned or challenged without triggering the full deterrent power of the surveillance state—the enforcement arm of the neoliberal financial order. This is a mode of predatory capitalism that presents itself as a universal social formation without qualification, a social form encircled by ideological and political certainty, and a cultural practice that replaces open civic powers with a closed set of consumer choices. As a result, corporate predation is emerging as a normalized form of low-intensity ambient violence that is conscripting all political differences, viable alternatives, and counter-readings of the world into the service of a financial elite and a savage form of Social Darwinism.

Despite their increasing ubiquity, the current mechanisms of diversion and their hidden order of politics have received some scrutiny. Robert Reich, for one, has asserted that any debate about the national debt should not only be about the broader issue of inequality but also should address crucial political questions regarding the increasing concentration of power and "entrenched wealth at the top."[8] We also see deeper analysis in Frank Rich's insistence that the endless debate conducted largely in the mainstream media about Washington being dysfunctional misses the point. Rich argues that behind the media's silly argument that both parties are to blame for the current deadlock lies a Republican Party strategy to make the federal government look as dysfunctional as possible so as to convince the wider American public that the government should be dismantled and its services turned over to for-profit private interests. In fact, a number of recent critics now believe that the extremist nature of the current Republican Party represents one of the most difficult obstacles to any viable form of governance. Thomas E. Mann and Norman J. Ornstein, two prominent conservative commentators, have recently argued that not only have moderates been pushed out of the Republican Party, but they are for all intents and purposes "virtually extinct." Mann and Ornstein go even further by stating:

> In our past writings, we have criticized both parties when we believed it was warranted. Today, however, we have no choice but to acknowledge that the core of the problem lies with the Republican Party. The GOP has become an insurgent outlier in American politics. It is ideologically extreme; scornful of compromise; unmoved by conventional understanding of facts, evidence and science; and dismissive of the legitimacy of its political opposition. When one party moves this far from the mainstream, it makes it nearly impossible for the political system to deal constructively with the country's challenges.[9]

Robert F. Kennedy Jr., has further emphasized the dire effects of extremist politics on democracy, describing the Republican Party's "corporate-centric super-PACs as treasonous." He states that Americans are "now in a free fall toward old-fashioned oligarchy; noxious, thieving and tyrannical." With the most corporate-friendly Supreme Court since the Gilded Age having passed the Citizens United decision, "those who have the money now have the loudest voices in our democracy while poor Americans are mute."[10]

In addition, a tradition of progressive intellectuals has long alerted the public to the decades-long transformation of the United States from a weak democracy to a spirited authoritarian state. Noam Chomsky, Judith Butler, Chris Hedges, Angela Davis, Sheldon Wolin, Stanley Aronowitz, Robert Scheer, Robin D. G. Kelley, Matt Taibbi, Susan George, and David Theo Goldberg, among others, have challenged the permanent war economy, the erosion of civil liberties, the moral bankruptcy of the liberal intelligentsia, the corporate control of the media, the criminal wars of repression abroad, the rise of the torture state, and the increasing militarization of everyday life.

This critical tradition is important because it links cultural forces to current politics in ways that reveal a larger, more powerful system operating behind and within the partisan theater played out in the Capitol. If one argues against the extremism embraced by the Republican Party—with its ongoing war on women, immigrants, young people, impoverished communities, voting rights, and all manner of civil rights—this should not suggest that the Democratic Party occupies a valued liberal position. On the contrary, policy in the United States is now being shaped by a Democratic Party that has become increasingly more conservative in the last thirty years, along with a Republican Party that now represents one of the most extreme political forces ever to wield power in Washington. And while the Republican Party has fallen into the hands of radical extremists, both parties "support shifting the costs of the crisis and the government bail-outs of banks, large corporations, and the stock market, onto the mass of the citizens."[11] Both parties support bailing out the rich and taking huge donations from and doing the bidding of massive corporations. Moreover, both parties reject the idea of democracy as a collectively inhabited public space and ethos that unconditionally stands for civilian-centered, community-driven, non-authoritarian set of rights, values, and processes for sustaining and advancing a free and open society. President Obama and his Wall Street advisors may hold on to some weak notion of the social contract, but they are far from liberal when it comes to embracing the military physics of the corporate warfare state.

As Chris Hedges, Paul Street, Noam Chomsky, and Salvatore Babones have repeatedly pointed out, calling attention to the Republican Party's extremism should not cloud the increasingly authoritarian positions endorsed by the Obama administration. For instance, President Obama has deported more immigrants than his predecessor George W. Bush; he has advocated for the privatization of public schools, pursued neoliberal modes of educational governance, and slashed funds from a number of vital social service programs. He has put into place a health care program that eliminated the public option and joined forces with insurance companies and Big Pharma.

As is well known, the Obama administration has also kept Guantánamo open, justified warrantless wiretapping, accelerated drone attacks that killed many innocent civilians, supported indefinite detention, and sanctioned a form of "extraordinary rendition" in which potential terrorists are abducted and shipped off to foreign countries to be tortured.[12] In fact, the realm of politics has moved so far to the right in the United States that modes of extremism that were once thought unthinkable now appear moderate and commonplace. As Glenn Greenwald has argued, the USA PATRIOT Act, state-sponsored torture and assassinations, kill lists and surveillance programs, once "widely lamented as a threat to core American liberties," have "become such a fixture in our political culture that we are trained to take them for granted, to view the warped as normal."[13] Yet, while both parties have given up the mantel of democratic politics, the Republican Party is more outspoken in its range of targets and its zealous attempts to destroy those modes of governance and public spheres that provide the conditions for robust and critical forms of civic life, education, agency, and democracy.

Ideological Extremism and the Destruction of Democracy

The extremism of the current Republican Party has many political, ideological, economic, and cultural registers, but one of its most dangerous and punitive is its attack on the social state, the public good, and the very notion of responsible civilian government. If the Democratic Party has undermined vital civil liberties while promoting a warfare state, the Republican Party has created a new understanding of politics as the space in which corporations and finance capital provide the template for all aspects of governance and policy. Governance in this mode of politics is beholden to corporate power rather than to citizens, who increasingly come under the control of state apparatuses of punishment, including the courts, military, and police. If a slavish obedience to the corporate and finance state is visible in the Republican Party's call for deregulation, privatization, free trade, and a no-tax policy for the wealthy and corporations, then the rule of the carceral state becomes clear in its call for the criminalization of social issues, of intolerance of equal access for communities of color, of women's control of their own bodies, of public resources to assist the poor, and of free speech and protest.

While the use of military force against workers and civil rights has a long history in the United States, the dominance of finance capital is a more recent development and takes on a new urgency given the threat it currently poses to a substantive democracy. Robert McChesney argues that the supremacy of capital has transformed the United States from a weak democracy into a "Dollarocracy—the rule of money rather than the rule of people—a specifically U.S. form of plutocracy [which] is now so dominant, so pervasive, that it is accepted as simply the landscape people inhabit."[14] Michael Hudson extends this analysis by characterizing one element of the new extremism as a form of *financial warfare* waged against not merely the social state but all those groups that historically have fought for expanding political, economic, and personal rights. He writes:

Finance has moved to capture the economy at

large, industry and mining, public infrastructure (via privatization) and now even the educational system. (At over $1 trillion, U.S. student loan debt came to exceed credit-card debt in 2012). The weapon in this financial warfare . . . is to load economies (governments, companies and families) with debt, siphon off their income as debt service and then foreclose when debtors lack the means to pay. Indebting government gives creditors a lever to pry away land, public infrastructure and other property in the public domain. Indebting companies enable creditors to seize employee pension savings. And indebting labor means that it no longer is necessary to hire strikebreakers to attack union organizers and strikers. . . . In contrast to the promise of democratic reform nurturing a middle class a century ago, we are witnessing a regression to a world of special privilege in which one must inherit wealth in order to avoid debt and job dependency.[15]

As indicated above, a second feature of the new extremism is the ongoing privatization, commercialization, and destruction of public spaces. The impact of this attack on democratic public spheres should not be underestimated. Institutions of democratic culture such as schools, libraries, parks, the nonprofit sector, the art world, unions, the media, and other public spheres provide the spaces for critical thinking, informed dialogue, thoughtfulness, the affirmation of non-commodified norms, and the unconditional protection of social rights. They enable opportunities through which public values and important social issues are engaged, and they foster the conditions necessary for the development of an informed citizenry. But these public spheres, which continue to produce modes of critical reasoning and a collective ethos at odds with antidemocratic and market-driven values, are now viewed with disdain by the Republican Party. The new extremists are not simply wedded to a vicious anti-intellectualism; they scorn the very notion of reason and embrace ignorance as the foundation for community. This is evident in their rejection of the scientific method and reasoning, but also in their approval of fundamentalist positions that pander to ignorance as a basis for shutting down dissent, mobilizing supporters, and retooling American education as a business—as nothing more than a training site to initiate the young into a world where the corporate, financial, and military elite decide their needs, desires, and futures.

The third feature of the new extremism focuses on the attack on the social contract and welfare state and the ideas and institutions that make them possible. The new extremists recognize that opportunities to enact citizenship are as important as the idea of citizenship and they want to make sure that it is difficult, if not impossible, for the American public to learn and practice discourses of the common good, public life, and social justice—discourses in which a language for defending vital public spheres can be developed and taught. The Republican Party narratives of deficit and austerity are in reality an attempt to dismantle the welfare state and the social supports it provides. For Republican Party extremists, a hyperfocus on budget deficits becomes the key weapon in forcing the government to reduce its spending on Social Security, Medicare, Medicaid, and other social provisions at odds with market-driven values, deregulation, and the logic of privatization.

One consequence of this attack on the welfare state and the social contract has been the emergence of a market fundamentalism that trivializes democratic values and public concerns. At the same time, this market fundamentalism enshrines self over community, legitimates an all-embracing quest for profits, and promotes a Social Darwinism in which misfortune is seen as a weakness and the Hobbesian rule of a "war of all against all" replaces any vestige of shared responsibilities for others, the future, or the larger ecosystem on which all life depends. If the conservative revolution launched by Ronald Reagan and Margaret Thatcher had as its goal the rolling back of social democratic rights, the counterrevolutionaries who now control the Republican Party go much further: they are not interested in simply minimizing the role of the social state. They want to eliminate government-sponsored provisions, trade union rights, and other social and economic rights altogether. The enemy is a population empowered to defend and advance the public interest, community, and the environment through a substantive democracy designed to foster economic equality and social rights.

In this form of free-market fundamentalism, the new

authoritarianism elevates the unregulated and unfettered market to the status of idol or fetish and enforces the rule of finance as part of a larger project leading to a callous, corporate-dominated society. It also promotes an anti-public morality in which the only responsibility one has is to oneself, "with no responsibility for the interests or well-being of others."[16] How else to explain the refusal of both political parties to address the myriad of crises faced by young people that have turned youth between the ages of eighteen and twenty-four into the new face of the national homeless population? The growing plight of young people in America is revealed in the following poverty-related statistics: more than a million public school students are homeless in the United States, 57 percent of all children are in homes considered to be either low-income or impoverished, and half of all American children will be on food stamps at least once before they turn eighteen years old.[17]

At work here is the destruction of social and public values through a variety of strategies that John Clarke describes as "erasing the social" by withdrawing social protections for labor, "privatizing the social" by turning over publicly owned resources to profit-making interests, "subjugating the social" by subordinating social needs and policies to the imperatives of economic competitiveness and capitalist accumulation, "domesticating the social" by placing the burden for collective provision, security, and care solely on the family, and "narrowing the social" by downsizing it into "meaner, degraded or recitalist forms."[18] This new version of market fundamentalism displays little interest in preventing inequality from running out of control. In the mouths of political extremists, it supports a cruel ideology that feeds nicely into the notion that the social protections of the state have nothing to do with the common good or communal survival, but are largely a matter of charity.[19] Central to the subordination of the social is the spread of a belief system in which "individuals think of themselves in economic terms—as entrepreneurial, calculating selves whose world is structured through contractual or quasi-contractual relationships."[20] This leads to the next element of the new extremism.

The fourth feature of the new extremism is its use of the media and other cultural apparatuses to promote a neoliberal form of public pedagogy engaged in the production of identities, desires, and values that disparage any mode of sociality that supports the common good, public values, and shared responsibilities. The new extremism embraces a radical selfishness that celebrates a consumer-oriented person "whose actions reflect mostly their material self-interests."[21] This could be considered a form of *antipolitics*, an "authoritarian Utopia that is nothing less than 'a program of methodical destruction of collectives,' from trade unions and mill towns to families and small nations."[22] Under attack in this new authoritarianism are the social bonds and modes of community cohesion that enable individuals, families, neighborhoods, organizations, and social movements to resist the ongoing commercialization of everyday life, the deregulation of the economy, the corruption of politics, the massive increase in poverty, inequality, cruelty, and the emergence of a militarized surveillance state.

The new authoritarianism unleashes all the forces of a brutal self-absorption that deepens and expands both the structure of cruelty and its ongoing privatization. Unabashed self-interest has weakened any sense of collective purpose, just as America's obsession with radical individualism and wealth and the existence of gross inequality have become symptomatic of our ethical and material impoverishment.[23] As Bauman points out, "the consuming life is [now] lived as a supreme expression of autonomy," leaving no room for activity in the service of "commitment, devotion, [and] responsibility."[24] Social life in this anti-public discourse has little to do with democracy and the formative culture needed to nourish it. As public values are disdained and the very notions of the public good and civic imagination disappear, people surrender their citizenship. In turn, they are rendered disposable—becoming the waste products of a society increasingly wedded to throwing away not just consumer products, but human beings as well. What is new about the extremism that now rules American society is the *accelerating* decline of public values, now deemed irrelevant to the contemporary neoliberal order. A growing absence of public values weakens the foundation of social solidarity and creates identities, values, and desires that turn the principles of democracy against themselves, threatening to undermine the very possibility of politics as a democratic project.

The Suffocation of Imagination, Agency, and Hope
It is also critical to recognize that the war on the social contract, the welfare state, democratic politics, equality, and the

very idea of justice is more than an attack on social services, from Medicare to Social Security to the Equal Pay Act. More profoundly, it is an assault on "the basic architecture of our collective responsibility to ensure that Americans share in a decent life."[25] It is also an aggressive strike against the formative cultures and modes of individual and collective agency that engender a connection between the democratic polis and the possibility of economic, social, and political community. The new extremism and its politics of distraction draw attention away from serious social problems and the actual structural and ideological conditions that reproduce them. Underlying the shadow of authoritarianism is a corrosive attempt to produce a deep-felt cynicism and "loss of faith" in the ideals of justice and democracy.[26] To the degree that the private sphere becomes the only space in which to imagine any sense of hope, pleasure, or possibility, citizenship becomes distorted, removed from issues of equity, social justice, and civic responsibility. Tony Judt is right in arguing that we have entered a historical conjuncture in which politics is losing its shape, its power of attraction, and its ability to confront the antidemocratic pressures at work in American society today.[27]

Opposing the consolidation of authoritarian systems demands a new language for embracing social responsibility, defining the meaning of agency and politics, and revitalizing civic engagement. Rethinking the social means, in part, restoring the role of the state in providing regulations that limit the power of corporations and the financial service industries. It means reconfiguring the very nature of power in order to subordinate capitalism's major institutions to the rule of law, democratic values, and the precepts of justice and equality. The state is not merely an instrument of governance. It is a cultural site that produces and reflects the ethos of a society. Unfortunately, the U.S. government has largely relinquished democratic responsibility in favor of organized irresponsibility, promoting a culture in which ethics is privatized and separated from economic considerations, the rule of law can be used to produce legal illegalities, and politics operates in a realm set apart from the principles of justice, equality, and freedom. This suggests the need for the general population to organize social movements and advocate for modes of sovereignty at all levels of government in which *people* rather than money and corporations shape the nature of politics, policies, media, and the cultural institutions that provide the public values that nourish critical modes of citizenship and democracy itself.

The Role of Critical Education and Educated Hope in Taking Back Democracy

At stake here is more than a call for reform. The American public needs to organize around a revolutionary ideal that enables people to hold power, participate in the process of governing, and create public institutions and discourses capable of explaining and reversing chronic injustices evident everywhere in society. This is a revolution that not only calls for structural change, but also for a transformation in the ways in which subjectivities are created, desires are produced, and agency itself is safeguarded as crucial to any viable notions of community and freedom. There is a pedagogical element to rethinking the political that has often been ignored by progressives of various stripes. It is not enough to demand that people be restored their right to participate in the experience of governing. They must also be restored their right to be educated in every aspect of what it means to live and participate in a democracy-centered society. Pedagogy is necessarily central to the very meaning of politics, whether democratic or authoritarian. Democracy requires, at the very least, a type of education that fosters a working knowledge of citizenship and the development of individuals with the capacity to be self-reflective, passionate about the collective good, and able to defend the means by which ideas are translated into the worldly space of the public realm.[28]

The philosopher Cornelius Castoriadis surely is right when he asserts that we must take seriously the political task of creating those diverse public spheres that are capable of rendering all individuals fit to participate in the governing of society and willing to engage the social within a broader political and theoretical landscape, one that connects private interests to the common good rather than the priorities of corporate power and an endlessly commodifying, market-driven social order.[29] Democracy demands an informed citizenry, which can only be produced collectively through the existence of public spheres that give meaning to people's struggles for justice, economic rights, and human dignity. In that sense, resistance to the new authoritarianism in the United States might start with Castoriadis's insistence that any viable form of politics begins with creating the formative cultures and public spheres in which *critical education in the broadest sense* establishes the essential foundation and meaning of justice, social responsibility, and democracy. For Castoriadis, at the heart of such formative cultures are operative forms of public pedagogy that create citizens "who are critical thinkers capable of putting existing institutions into question so that democracy" can be nourished and sustained.[30] As a moral and political practice, pedagogy produces the knowledge, values, and identities that circulate in a particular society. *Critical forms of pedagogy*, therefore, become a determining factor in creating a society willing both to question itself and to struggle for those ideals that give meaning and life to the promise of a substantive democracy.

Against the dystopian visions that drive the new authoritarianism, there is a need for teachers, workers, artists, students, young people, academics, and others to produce a language of critique, provocation, and possibility. This is a discourse of civic engagement that embraces politics as a pedagogical practice organized, in part, around what I call *educated hope*. Educated hope sharpens the "ethopolitical" instrument and "operates at the root of where the ethical imagination and the political mingle."[31] Educated hope signals the merging of civic education and democratic action as part of a broader attempt to enable young people and others to take a critical stand in analyzing and transforming those values, ideologies, and market-driven politics that produce a growing machinery of inequality and social death. It suggests creating a new language and order of symbolic relations so as to understand the past as well as the dynamics of the present and the future.

Educators, progressives, and engaged citizens need a language that puts moral considerations back into the regressive culture of cost-benefit analysis and rejects the civic vacuum created by the extremist apostles of casino capitalism. We also need a language that is vigilant about not only where democratic identities are produced but also where forms of social agency are denied. Those concerned about the fate of justice and democracy need to reconfigure the political order in order to create relations of governance that are capable of addressing the increasing separation of national and local politics from the locus of power, which is now exercised on a global level and virtually unrestrained by nation-states. In other words, power is now global while politics is local. What this means is that globalization has loosened economic interests and military power from the political moorings that once anchored them to the nation-state. The traditional merging of power and politics as overseen by an electorate has been all but broken, and, as Bauman points out: "We may say that power has 'flown' from the historically developed institutions that used to exercise democratic control over uses and abuses of power in the modern nation-states. Globalization in its current form means a progressive disempowerment of nation-states and (so far) the absence of any effective substitute."[32]

Effective resistance to the new extremism in the United States must, therefore, be conceived as part of a broader planetary struggle, built on strong political and civic commitments and forms of solidarity that are both local and global in nature. Similarly, any viable challenge must move beyond critique and propose alternatives by rethinking the nature of what Jacques Derrida has called "the possible and impossible."[33] Thinking beyond the given involves constructing new narratives regarding the stories we tell about ourselves, our struggles, the future, and the promise of a democracy to come.

A language of critique and educated hope suggests a new and spirited struggle against a culture of civic illiteracy that permits the commanding institutions of society to be divorced from matters of ethics, social responsibility, and social cost. The new authoritarianism dominating American society, which attempts to make critical thinking irrelevant and reduce hope to a paralyzing cynicism, must be challenged by a politics and pedagogy that have the capacity not only to "influence those in power" but also to "mobilize those who don't have power."[34] This is a pedagogy that should "not only shift the way people think about the moment, but potentially energizes them to do something different."[35] A politics that merges critique and hope recognizes that while the idea of the good society may be under attack, it is far from being relegated to the dustbin of history.

With the grip of an authoritarian political culture and the politics of distraction getting stronger in American society, the current assault on democracy should be taken as an opportunity to generate new collective struggles in the hope of creating a future that refuses to be defined by the dystopian forces now shaping American society. In the aftermath of the massive suffering produced by World War II and the horrors of the Third Reich, Theodor W. Adorno refused to give up on hope as an essential condition of agency, politics, and justice. Writing under the shadow of an older form of authoritarianism, he insisted: "Thinking is not the intellectual reproduction of what already exists anyway. As long as it doesn't break off, thinking has a secure hold on possibility. Its insatiable aspect, its aversion to being quickly and easily satisfied, refuses the foolish wisdom of resignation. . . . Open thinking points beyond itself."[36] Adorno's words are both profound and instructive for the time in which we live because they point to the need to think beyond the given, to think beyond the distorted, market-based hope offered to us by the advocates of casino capitalism. Such thinking rooted in the radical imagination is a central goal of civic education, which, in the words of poet Robert Hass, is "to refresh the idea of justice which is going dead in us all the time."[37]

As long as there continues to be suffering in the world, individuals and social movements should, as Richard Swift points out, "take responsibility for the direction of society."[38] Ongoing talks about deficits, the debt ceiling, and the cutting back of social provisions should not be ignored because it is wrong-headed. Rather, it should be connected to broader antidemocratic practices and understood as posing a serious threat to a society now at risk of being dominated by religious and economic fundamentalists. The task facing the American public in this moment of government deceit and civic abandonment is to think beyond the parameters of the given, to recognize that we cannot *act* otherwise unless we can *think* otherwise. At stake here is the need to renew the relationships among hope, community, conscience, and democracy. If we are to overcome the debilitating pessimism of the current era, it is crucial to combine gritty realism with a sense of educated hope that taps into our deepest experiences, allowing us to take risks and to think beyond our current thinking. As Alain Badiou states, this is "a matter of showing how the space of the possible is larger than the one assigned—that something else is possible, but not that everything is possible."[39] Imagining the unimaginable necessitates asking crucial questions regarding what types of knowledge, politics, and moral order are necessary to sustain a vibrant democracy. What will it take to broaden our collective horizon of understanding in order to support the ongoing and always unfinished work of justice, democratization, and freedom?

THREE

HURRICANE SANDY AND THE POLITICS OF DISPOSABILITY

Crises are reputed to strike at random, but their consequences, and above all their long-term consequences, are class-managed. The severity of the crisis may result from the intensity of deregulation, but the harshness and pungency of their human effects stay stubbornly—and tightly—class controlled.[1]

—Zygmunt Bauman

In 2005, Hurricane Katrina revealed how specific populations were being systemically denied any consideration of human dignity and hope by those wielding power and authority in the United States. The heart-wrenching scenes of suffering and death endured by racialized communities, immigrants, the sick, and the elderly remain etched like ghostly traces in our collective memories surrounding Hurricane Katrina. In the wake of the October 2012 devastation wreaked by Hurricane Sandy on communities along the northeastern seaboard of the United States, it has become apparent that the victims of the storm will be denied the sustained national focus and compassion that produced the inward soul-searching arising from Katrina's human tragedy. Seven years hence, the response to Hurricane Sandy has demonstrated how the politics of disposability exposed by Katrina have been normalized, despite the ongoing impacts of brutalizing forms of racial exclusion, misery, deprivation, suffering, and collective punishment. It has become clear that Americans have once again entered the thick fog of historical amnesia in which memories of violence against those considered disposable have disappeared from the registers of deep-seated public and ethical concern.

The floodwaters driven by Hurricane Sandy that ravaged the east coast of the United States undeniably reveal that the ecological crisis triggered by global warming is no longer an issue of possibility in the future, it is a fact in the present which is directly strengthened by market-driven forces that plunder the environment and obstruct attempts to reverse the flood of carbon emissions released by big business.

But the fundamental lesson of Hurricane Sandy is not to be found in the lack of disaster preparedness on the part of many cities, the race and class divisions at work in urban areas, the crisis of global warming, or the ways in which the rich and powerful used the destruction produced by Sandy to call for neoliberal reforms, though these factors deserve our consideration. Rather, it is found in the emerging dystopia, fashioned as much by natural disasters as by political catastrophes, that reveals the increasing level of acceptable violence, surveillance, and authoritarian aggression perpetrated against those populations now viewed as unproductive, expendable, and disposable.[2]

When, following Hurricane Katrina, images of dead

bodies floating in the flood waters of New Orleans materialized in national media alongside a sound track of desperate cries for help from thousands of black, brown, elderly, and medically ailing people, they revealed a vulnerable and destitute segment of the nation's citizenry—one which conservatives not only had refused to see as such, but indeed had spent the better part of three decades demonizing. In the aftermath of Katrina, the nightmarish images of the abandoned, desperate, and vulnerable would not go away. They called out to the collective conscience of Americans, demanding answers to questions that had finally been asked about those communities of people who have been excluded from the American dream and abandoned to their own limited resources in the midst of a major natural disaster.

But that moment of national introspection that held the promise of real social change too soon passed when the United States faced another disaster in 2008 as the country plunged into a period of acute turmoil ushered in by bankers' acts of economic mass destruction—predatory loans, financial fraud, foreclosure abuse—perpetrated against millions of Americans, and ultimately against the nation as a whole.[3] As a consequence, as the rich still got richer, widespread hardship and suffering soon bore down on vast numbers of lower-middle- and working-class Americans who would lose their jobs, their homes, their health care, their life savings, their sense of security, and their hope for the future. Yet the corporate media have conveniently overlooked the connection between market-driven financial policy and market-driven disaster response.[4] And criminal bankers, unlike those who protest their financial atrocities, get away without the humiliation of handcuffs, arrest, jail, or prison.

In 2014, a report from Michael E. Horowitz, the inspector general of the Justice Department, stated that mortgage-related fraud—corporate crime—was never a high priority for nation's top law enforcement agency, because it is simply unequipped or unwilling to combat complex financial frauds, and "that there will be few consequences for those who commit financial fraud in the future."[5] Acknowledging that "complex financial crimes were the lowest priority for the criminal investigative division," the *New York Times* emphasized that the report pointed to an egregious flight from political responsibility on the part of the U.S. government and reinforced the conception that "that there really are two levels of justice in this country, one for the people with power and money and one for everyone else."[6]

The notion that the government is indifferent, if not politically aligned, with predatory financial elites should come as no surprise, but what is disturbing is that the call for criminal prosecution of Wall Street criminals does not go far enough and is often used by liberals to shut down any further debate about to restructure our predatory financial system."[7] Arresting, jailing, and prosecuting financial predators en masse would, in fact, be a substantive victory for economic justice and for preventing future financial crimes against the nation. As a victory of public accountability, it would also send the right message toward preventing botched government/corporate response to natural and political catastrophes such as those witnessed in response to Hurricane Sandy. But such actions do not go far enough.

Hurricane Sandy not only failed to arouse a heightened sense of moral outrage and call for justice, it was quickly, if not seamlessly, woven into a narrative of denial surrounding those larger economic and political forces, mechanisms, and technologies by which certain populations, when exposed to a natural catastrophe, are treated like waste. One reason for this case of historical amnesia and ethical indifference may lie in the emerging vicissitudes of an era eager to balk at— rather than to immediately decrease—the impact of human activity on climate change, an era in which violent weather has become normalized alongside all the other forms of ambient violence that seem to circumscribe our everyday lives.

These days Americans are quickly uninterested in news of catastrophes that are not at their own doorstep. Major natural disasters and their consequences are now framed through the vocabulary of fate or the unyielding script of personal tragedy, conveniently allowing an ethically cleansed American public to ignore the sordid violence and suffering such circumstances heap upon those already impoverished populations caught in the silent grip of intergenerational deprivation, exploitation, and hardship.

It gets worse. Catastrophe is no longer simply normalized; it is often rendered into a dramatic spectacle fit for TV and other entertainment products. Rather than being analyzed within broader social categories such as power, politics, poverty, race, class, and the need for change, the violence produced by natural disasters is now highly individualized and mostly limited to human interest stories about loss and individual suffering. Questions concerning how the violence of Hurricane Sandy impacted differently those groups marginalized by race, age, sickness, and class were downplayed or ignored. Lost in both the immediacy of the recovery efforts and the public discourse circulated by most of the mainstream media were the abandoned fates and needless suffering of residents in public housing apartments from Red Hook to the Lower East Side to the poorest sections of the Rockaway Peninsula and other neglected areas along the New Jersey shoreline. Many of these areas had *already* suffered from another kind of catastrophe long before Sandy ravaged their neighborhoods. This was an economic and social catastrophe arising from persistent impoverishment, denial of proper health care, unemployment, and inadequate housing. Underlying factors of power, force, and privilege were removed from accounts of the reconstruction efforts following Sandy, just as questions of politics gave way to a flood of human interest stories on CNN, NBC, CBS, and nightly news programs.

Violence against the other—whether as a result of a natural or a human-made catastrophe—has been removed from any viable moral compass, even as the horizon of public values and social justice has darkened in the United States. The essential ethical grammar of minimizing human suffering now appears quaint, and the consequences have been especially profound for the already disadvantaged—those ever expanding and increasingly visible populations of disposable people whose lives and communities are wantonly destroyed and seemingly beyond salvage. In the aftermath of Sandy, zones of privilege in New York City and other areas hit hard by the storm benefited from an immediate government response and seemed to return to business as usual within a few weeks. Yet, as Nick Pinto points out, "weeks after the storm, many New Yorkers in storm-damaged neighborhoods had yet to see any sort of institutional relief at all [and as] the days stretched into weeks and thousands of people continued to live with the basic necessities . . . it became clear that the storm had only exacerbated and laid bare the fissures of inequality that already riddled New York."[8] Many of the victimized, whose political voices and social visibility have been so often disregarded, were not merely dissatisfied with the failure of the government to come to their aid. They felt abandoned, and rightly so. Although it has become an indisputable reality that inequality is one of the most significant factors making certain groups vulnerable to storms and other types of disasters, differences in income, wealth, power, and geography rarely informed the mainstream media analyses of the massive destruction and suffering caused by Sandy.[9] The stark truth bears repeating: out of 150 countries, the United States has the fourth highest wealth disparity.[10] As Joseph Stiglitz points out: "Nowadays, these numbers show that the American dream is a myth. There is less equality of opportunity in the United States today than there is in Europe—or, indeed, in any advanced industrial country for which there are data."[11] A 2014 Oxfam study found that 85 people own as much as half of the world's population. In the United States, just 400 families have wealth and assets approximately equivalent to the bottom 50 percent of the country's people.[12]

Inequality and social disparities are not simply about the concentration of wealth in the hands of an elite 1 percent. The unequal use of power, the shaping of policies in terms of market interests, and the privileging of a conservative, wealthy minority that has accumulated vast amounts of wealth—all of these have contributed to social marginalization and a growing income gap between the rich and the poor. And America is paying a high price for its shameful levels of inequality. Manhattan, one of the epicenters of the storm's savagery, has extreme levels of inequality that not only stand out in the United States but rival parts of sub-Saharan Africa.[13] The chronic suffering produced by such economic injustice is revealed in the lack of housing options for the impoverished and the fact that New York City shelters "more homeless people than any city in the United States: a record 47,000 women, men and children, in a system strained to the breaking point."[14] At the time of this writing, New York City shelters 22,000 children who have no home, hundreds of whom live in "shelters that inspectors have repeatedly cited for deplorable conditions."[15] Within this geography of massive income and wealth inequality, "the wealthiest 20 percent of Manhattan residents make $391,022" on average each year, while the "poorest 20 percent made only $9,681."[16]

Devastation comes in many forms and has numerous causes, but it rarely garners public attention unless it is the result of terrorism or natural causes, such as hurricanes, severe flooding, droughts, tornados, tsunamis, and other such events. Even then, often erased from consideration are those correctable forms of devastation such as impoverishment of whole communities, mass foreclosure, deep-seated inequality, market-driven systems that hijack the public, "free-market economic policies based on de-regulation and hyper excessive privatization of resources," chronic environmental degradation, and the control of economic and political power by a small elite.[17] Similarly, matters of agency, if not survival itself, are left disconnected from not only the privileges of wealth and power, but also their underside—the vulnerability and powerlessness that come with economic deprivation and denial of resources. Nevertheless, how disasters unfold through relations of power ultimately challenges the myth that major catastrophes are the great equalizers that affect everyone. They may affect everyone, but not in the same way. Naomi Klein makes clear the many protections conferred by wealth and status in the context of a disaster:

> In the past six years, we have seen the emergence of private firefighters in the United States, hired by insurance companies to offer a "concierge" service to their wealthier clients, as well as the short-lived "HelpJet"—a charter airline in Florida that offered five-star evacuation services from hurricane zones [whose ad shamelessly stated]: "No standing in lines, no hassle with crowds, just a first class experience that turns a problem into a vacation." And, post-Sandy, upscale real estate agents

are predicting that back-up power generators will be the new status symbol with the penthouse and mansion set.[18]

For all those affected by Hurricane Sandy, wealth mattered in a number of ways that exacerbated the storm's devastation. The privileged elite could draw from savings or strong credit to move into hotels, fly out of town, take off from work, pay for immediate tree removal and emergency responses, buy electric generators, etc. Not so for those who lacked wealth or resources. The area's poor—often caricatured as parasites feeding on the body politic—had to stay behind because they lacked the means to move, while the working class provided the infrastructure for fighting fires, policing the streets, cooking food in the city's elite restaurants, driving taxis, providing door services, and taking care of the children of the rich. As David Rohde observed, "the city's cooks, doormen, maintenance men, taxi drivers, and maids left their loved ones at home."[19] David Caruso further elaborated on the state of the sick and frail in the aftermath of Sandy. He wrote:

> Some of society's most vulnerable people—the elderly, the disabled and the chronically ill—have been pushed to the brink in the powerless, flood-ravaged neighborhoods struggling to recover from Superstorm Sandy. The storm didn't just knock out electricity and destroy property when it came ashore in places like the Far Rockaway section of

Queens. It disrupted the fragile support networks that allowed the neighborhood's frailest residents to get by. Here, the catastrophe has closed pharmacies, kept home care aids from getting to elderly clients and made getting around in a wheelchair impossible. The city has recorded at least two deaths of older men in darkened buildings.[20]

Hurricane Sandy did more than expose New York City's vulnerabilities; it also exposed its economic divide and revealed a new acceptance of disposability. This became particularly clear when certain populations in Manhattan received aid more quickly than others during the post-Sandy reconstruction efforts.

In a society that exalts individual celebrity and fame, and radiates a sociopathic lack of interest in community, compassion, and other non-market values, it is not surprising that those left behind in some parts of New York City and other areas were barely visible, banished to private orbits of self-reliance. Hardly a mention was made of the first responders who lost their homes in Breezy Point or the poor elderly who were trapped for days in housing projects "facing cold temperatures, food shortages," electrical failures, piles of uncollected and exposed trash, and lack of proper medical care.[21] While it became clear that Lower Manhattan was a low priority for receiving government and private relief efforts, neither its inhabitants' vulnerability nor the iniquitous treatment they were accorded were factored into post-Sandy mainstream media coverage.[22] Yet, ultimately,

Sandy laid bare what many people did not want to see: a throwaway society that appears all too willing to extend its endless cycle of material waste to the production and disposal of human lives. What became clear in the aftermath of the storm was that there are groups of people whose lives are for the most part considered "unreal" and who occupy an invisible space where their hardships are rarely seen or heard by the broader society.

For those in some areas of New York City, such as Brooklyn and entire towns along the New Jersey shoreline, class lines were readily exposed as emergency aid was either slow or barely existent.[23] Long before Hurricane Sandy hit the densely populated eastern seaboard, scientists had warned that thousands of poor people living in vulnerable coastal regions needed to be protected from such a storm.[24] But the events surrounding Sandy registered more than incompetence, a lack of compassion, and ignorance in response to such warnings. They were the consequence of a systemic, violent form of social engineering in which those populations in the United States marginalized by class and race are forced to negotiate their fate alone, reduced to a state of terminal exclusion, and banished to the far edges of the ethical imagination.

What needs to be recognized is that at the root of the problems that hampered relief efforts for the poor following Hurricane Sandy is *politics*. Even natural disasters are never far removed from politics. As Joseph Stiglitz points out in another context, politics "is where the rules of the game are made, that is where we decide on policies that favor the rich."[25] And it is precisely because we we have been indoctrinated by an authoritarian social order wedded to the destruction of the social state, social protections, and the social contract that very idea of disposable populations—even when seen—no longer seems capable of shocking us or shaming us. Corporate predation, enforced by state violence and public neglect have been successfully normalized.

The stories that a society tells about itself are often a measure of how it imagines itself, how it values democracy, and how it anticipates its future. Such stories become integral not only to how people see themselves, but also how a society determines which lives are worth living, what modes of agency count, what lives matter, and what deaths should be grieved. Hurricane Sandy was a natural disaster that produced enormous damage, pain, and suffering for millions of Americans. People living in poor, densely populated, urban, and coastal areas went for weeks without power, electricity, water, heat, and shelter. The emergency response involved faltering attempts by the Obama administration to affirm the government's responsibility to its citizens by protecting the victims of the hurricane from the savage caprices of nature. Not only did the U.S. Federal Emergency Management Agency (FEMA) provide inadequate financial assistance to many residents who had lost their homes, but the Republican leadership in the House of Representatives needlessly delayed passing legislation that would have provided billions of dollars to Hurricane Sandy relief efforts for New Jersey and New York.[26]

Within the days, weeks, and months following Hurricane Sandy, the human costs of this natural catastrophe on those populations considered disposable became more visible and visceral as a result of the failure of recovery efforts to address their dire needs and suffering. At the same time, an elitist spectacle of cruelty surfaced among government officials and the dominant media that both legitimated and accelerated the view that specific groups did not deserve the government aid and relief provided through emergency recovery efforts, at least not in the most pressing sense.

Within this regime of authoritarian control and violence, the politics of disposability is shored up by the assumption that some lives and social relationships are not worthy of kindness, not worthy of a meaningful social existence, not worthy of assistance. This neoliberal culture of cruelty is fueled by a collapse of public values and the belief that all social bonds not articulated through money—and the power that money buys—are ignorable. Economic competition, capital accumulation, celebrity, and self-interest are now openly embraced as the most important forces shaping all aspects of society. In this unscrupulous discourse, disposable populations and the economic and social hardships they experience are attributed to individualized forms of moral bankruptcy. Lacking social protections, such populations increasingly are targeted by the growing reach of the punishing state, reduced to being a source of entertainment, or relegated to what Étienne Balibar calls the "death zones of humanity," where they are rendered superfluous and subject to a mode of "production for elimination."[27]

In a culture defined by excessive inequality, suffering,

and cruelty, the protective covering of the state along with the public values and the formative culture necessary for a functioning democracy are corrupted.[28] As Bauman has suggested, disposable populations exist in "a condition of 'liminal drift'"; such people are reduced to being "outcasts and outlaws," stripped of basic necessities even as their identities are burdened with the language and reality of debt, survival, and redundancy.[29] And the disposable are not merely those populations subjected to extreme impoverishment. Increasingly they are individuals and groups now ravaged by bad mortgages, poor credit, and huge debt. They are the growing army of the unemployed forced to abandon their houses, credit cards, and ability to consume—a liability that pushes them to the margins of a market society. These are the groups whose homes will not be covered by insurance, who have no place to live, and no resources to fall back on. They have no ways to imagine how the problems they are facing are not just personal issues, but deeply structural in nature, built into a system that views the social contract and the welfare state as manifestations of a contagious disease. At the same time that an increasing number of Americans silently lose their jobs, their health coverage, their credit and their future, bankers fiercely defend the inequality that their massive income and bonuses flaunt. For example, in an interview with the *Wall Street Journal*, Robert Benmosche, the chief executive of the American International Group, "compares the uproar over bonuses to lynchings in the Deep South—the real kind, involving murder—and declared that the bonus backlash 'just as bad and just as wrong.' "[30]

This type of ethical obscenity is scripted and played out within a larger theater of authoritarian cruelty, becoming a form of intellectual violence that provides legitimation and justification for entire communities to be reduced to the misery of a kind of social death—lives immobilized by crippling inequalities, deprivations, and disciplinary regulations. Both immediately before and after Hurricane Sandy decimated the eastern seaboard, it became possible to take a shocking glimpse at the larger ideological, political, and governmental mechanisms currently at work in the United States. A disciplinary machinery and vocabulary had already been created in which certain subjects become invisible, expelled to zones of abandonment. Within this neoliberal discourse of greed, avarice, and cruelty, social and communal bonds of trust and compassion are shredded; human suffering becomes an object of indifference, if not disdain; and the privileged elite, their lobbyists, front groups and media platforms attack advocates of social responsibility, justice, and protest. Evidence of the discourse of disposability was apparent in the ways in which the issue of poverty had been "nearly invisible in U.S. media coverage of the 2012 election" just before superstorm Sandy struck. [31] The disintegration of public values and collective memory loomed large as matters of inequality, collective hardship, and collective suffering were stored out of sight in some dark recess of organized forgetting—in spite of the fact that in the United States "46 million people, or 15.1 percent of the population [along with] more than one in five children (22 percent) live in poverty, as do more than a quarter of all blacks (27 percent) and Latinos (26 percent)."[32]

A callous indifference to the plight of the impoverished was also made clear in the remarks of former presidential candidate Mitt Romney in his derogatory reference to the 47 percent of adult Americans who don't pay income taxes for one reason or another as "people who believe that they are victims, who believe the government has a responsibility to care for them, who believe that they are entitled to health care, to food, to housing, to you-name-it."[33] In a post-election comment, Romney reproduced this logic when telling a group of his financial backers that Obama won the election because he gave policy gifts to specific interest groups, "especially the African American community, the Hispanic community and young people."[34] In this instance, Romney simply affirmed Newt Gingrich's more overtly racist claim that President Obama was a "food stamp president . . . who was comfortable sending a lot of people checks for doing nothing."[35] Right-wing pundits such as Bill O'Reilly, Rush Limbaugh, Sarah Palin, and Sean Hannity offered up additional examples of the discourse of disposability and culture of cruelty by claiming that 47 percent "want things" and are welfare moochers and "wards of the state."[36]

But this economic Darwinist measure of human value is not limited to right-wing politicians, pundits, conservative media apparatuses, or a Republican Party that is now in the hands of extremists. The discourse of disposability—whereby those marginalized by race and class are deemed to be economic drains on society and unworthy of social benefits—is also built into liberal governmental policy. This was made particularly clear when former Mayor Michael

Bloomberg was willing to divert scarce resources for Hurricane Sandy storm relief such as food, power generators, and public services to the New York City Marathon rather than provide them to the hardest hit victims of the hurricane, especially residents in Staten Island. Alex Koppelman writing in *The New Yorker* captured both the extent of the resources that would have been wasted on the marathon and why it should have been immediately canceled:

> [T]he amount of *stuff* available to the organization that puts on the marathon, the New York Road Runners [N.Y.R.R.], that could instead have gone to helping people struggling after the storm is stunning. The *New York Post* has already noted the massive portable generators set up in Central Park, which, the *Post* says, are big "enough to power 400 homes in ravaged areas like Staten Island, the Rockaways and downtown Manhattan." And that's just the beginning. At the start of a typical race, sponsor Poland Spring provides more than ninety thousand eight-ounce bottles of water, plus more than sixty thousand gallons more along the way. That water could have gone to the people in Breezy Point, or to those getting water from hydrants, or those without any at all. Or the N.Y.R.R. could have relinquished the twenty-five hundred portable toilets it will put in place on Sunday, giving people without running water some dignity, or at least a way to save their drinking water for

drinking, rather than flushing. The Bowery Mission, a shelter in Lower Manhattan, is asking for donations of iced tea and Gatorade as an alternative to serving only water to its clients. Presumably other shelters are asking the same thing. Maybe N.Y.R.R. could have spared some of the thirty thousand or so gallons of Gatorade it distributes each year? And surely there are people out there who, after a very long week, would have appreciated even one of the cans of beer earmarked for the pre-race dinner, out of the eighteen thousand cans provided last year?[37]

Focusing on the marathon rather than the city's poor and storm relief, Bloomberg made clear that his first priority was offering up a recreational spectacle that would distract attention from the plight of the city's poorest residents. What Bloomberg did not expect was the populist rage that followed, especially from Staten Island where the race was scheduled to begin. As Alan Woods noted:

While thousands of families in devastated neighborhoods had no power, the people could see hundreds of generators lying idly behind barbed wire barriers awaiting the arrival of the marathon runners. This one gesture summed up in people's minds all the arrogant contempt that the wealthy elite have towards the majority. One indignant woman said of the Mayor: "He is sitting in there

warm and dry while we are out here freezing our
butts off. He is delusional!"[38]

In the face of public anger, Bloomberg eventually canceled the event but not before he had made obvious the
message that, as Chris Hedges points out, those who are
poor and voiceless are expendable, "a drain on efficiency
and progress. They are viewed as refuse. And as refuse . . .
have no voice and no freedom. . . . This is a world where
only corporate power and profit are sacred. It is a world of
barbarism."[39]

The cruelty unleashed by neoliberal acolytes was further highlighted when a number of right-wing policy advocates argued in various mainstream news sources that the
destruction wreaked by Sandy provided an excellent opportunity for privatizing the Natural Flood Insurance Program
and eliminating labor protections, among other regulations
that might hamper the superrich from using the disaster to
rake in big profits. One brazen, if not ruthless, suggestion
from right-wing economist Russell S. Sobel in a *New York
Times* online forum argued that the most devastated areas
caused by Hurricane Sandy provided a chance for FEMA to
establish "free trade zones—in which all normal regulations,
licensing and taxes [would be] suspended [and would] better
provide the goods and services victims need."[40] This was only
somewhat less extreme than an earlier suggestion by Mitt
Romney that FEMA should actually be abolished in order to
allow the private sector to take over disaster management.[41]

The lessons of Hurricane Sandy raise serious questions

not only about the economic and racial divides that characterize the United States and the seriousness of current corporate practices that are destabilizing weather patterns and destroying the biosphere, but also about the exercise of neoliberal power that escapes any sense of moral responsibility and is answerable only to money—those who have it and use it to control both policy and the population. As neoliberalism spreads across the globe, there seems to be little that governments can do in fulfilling a broad central commitment to their citizens. This suggests that the American public must become all the more attentive to what populations are being protected and what populations are being dehumanized or ignored. Acts of exclusion, forms of social death, and what Hedges calls "sacrifice zones" are proliferating at a rapid pace in the United States.[42] These are the places of social abandonment where Americans are trapped in interminable cycles of poverty, powerlessness, and hopelessness as a direct result of changeable policies that enforce capitalistic greed and allow individuals, families, communities, and ecosystems to be all but "destroyed for quarterly profit."[43] A necessary step toward reversing these trends involves a systemic reassertion of public values and institutions, both of which are currently under intense attack.

The assault on public values and at-risk communites is carried out on multiple fronts and is ideologically normalized through multiple methods. One such method is through the proliferation of Hollywood films that serve a propaganda function, such as the anti-public education movie *Won't Back Down*, which are largely funded by a slew of billionaires such as Bill Gates and Philip Anschutz. *Won't Back Down* serves as an advertisement for charter schools by portraying and denigrating public schools as utter failures due to the dysfunctionality of unions and the incompetence of public school teachers.[44] The lesson here is that public values have no place in school reform.

The assault on public values is also evident in a media landscape that mirrors commercial culture's celebration of wealth and violence, and its glaring non-representation of huge sectors of the population: indigenous nations, communities of color, immigrants, activists and other people of conscience. Equally deplorable is the proliferation of a dominant screen culture, extending from video games and Internet sites to blockbuster films and television programs, that encourages immersion in a rush of gratuitous spectacles of violence that offer a kind of adrenalized exhilaration from the suffering of others. America is immersed in a culture of violence, one which becomes all the more dangerous as the notion of moral conscience, like the notion of social agency, seems all but forgotten. This was strikingly evident after the tragic deaths of twenty young children and six educators shot and killed at Sandy Hook Elementary School in Newtown, Connecticut. In the aftermath of the shootings, gun sales increased dramatically and the National Rifle Association insisted that the response to such violence should be arming teachers and putting more guns in schools, proving once again that guns are not merely tools in America, but "an object of reference"[45] that testifies to "the attractive power of deadly violence itself."[46]

The atrophy of public values and civic imagination are also on display in the privatization of language, morality, and everyday life.[47] Trapped in an unwillingness to translate private troubles into broader social considerations, the discourse of social protections is reduced to the vocabulary of charity and individual giving. In the aftermath of Hurricane Sandy, the overly washed elite of New York City was discovering poverty while exoticizing the poor. Sarah Maslin Nir pointed critically to the elite's fascination with poverty porn by noting its "voyeuristic interest in the plight of the poor, treating [their trip into disaster areas] as an exotic weekend outing." [48] She also noted the complaint of a resident of a Rockaway project who stood by "as volunteers snapped iPhone photos of her as she waited in line for donated food and clothing."[49] The implications of being photographed were not lost on the Rockaway resident, who commented that she and her friends felt as if they were "in a zoo."[50]

The obsessive pursuit of self-interest is fortified through an equally compulsive refusal of critical analysis, dissent, and the formative culture essential to the conditions for a sustainable democracy. Critical thinking, dialogue, and thoughtfulness have been expunged from America's national vocabulary as diverse forms of market fundamentalism wage a war against reason, democracy, and public values. But anti-intellectualism and moral indifference are not limited to the ideological conventions of mainstream media, or even to the widespread economic and religious fundamentalisms that now heavily shape the U.S. government, including both its domestic and its foreign policy decisions. The intellectual protocols of inquiry and critical questioning seem to be disappearing wholesale from American culture, along with the ethical assessments needed to make visible the intense suffering sweeping across the United States like an out-of-control wildfire.[51]

The war on democracy and people's democratic rights is the same war being waged against ecological sustainability and must be linked to the relentless drive not only to commodify all aspects of everyday life, but to commodify the planet.[52] Privatization not only increases the likelihood of the disappearance of those considered disposable. As a discourse, it also reinforces a stripped-down notion of responsibility, which in turn alleviates the weight of moral conscience and social obligations. It undermines and destroys, whenever possible, those modes of social agency, collective structures, and bonds of sociality capable of holding power accountable, resisting the antidemocratic pressures of neoliberalism, and imagining visions that prioritize an investment in the public good over visions of happiness characterized by an endless search for immediate gratification. In a society in which "markets are detached from morals" and a market economy easily transforms into a market society, market values increasingly shape areas of everyday life where they do not belong.[53] As markets provide the only template through which to address society's needs, money becomes the ultimate measure of one's worth, while consuming becomes the ultimate index of what it means to invest in one's identity, relations with others, and larger society.

As social rights and other non-market values are rendered irrelevant, those who openly pursue them as forms critique or protest are immediately considered aberrant to security—suspects to monitored, deterred or criminalized, removed from any kind of ethical grammar that would acknowledge those economic, political, and social forces that produce their suffering and marginalization. As Jonathan Simon points out, the punishing state chooses to spend its money on discipline rather than social support: the result is a "governing through crime" ethos and a punishment culture that "allows government intervention in areas of American life that once seemed to have nothing to do with criminals."[54] Everything from public schools and social service agencies to sports events are infused with a punishing ethic and a primitive militarism. The war on terror has likewise morphed into a war on civil liberties, a war on immigrants, and a war on privacy. The crucial questions of what "effectively goes on in our culture, or what kind of society is emerging here" are dissolved in a culture of civic illiteracy, punitiveness, cruelty, and malice.[55] One consequence is that there has been a shift in social affairs toward the criminalization of social problems and dissent. Institutions once meant to abolish human suffering now produce it, magnifying the historic prejudices and racism that continue to burden American society.[56] For example, three-strikes sentencing laws have "created a cruel, Kafkaesque criminal justice system that [has] lost all sense of proportion, doling out life sentences disproportionately to black defendants."[57] We are living through what psychologist Robert Jay Lifton rightly calls a "death-saturated age" in which matters of violence, survival, and trauma now infuse everyday life.[58]

Such antidemocratic forces are not new, but they have been intensified and deepened under expanding neoliberal policies. They have also been reconfigured in more power-ful and lethal ways through a frontal assault on the social contract, the welfare state, and social protections.[59] Positive visions of the good society and the importance of public val-ues and civic life are being destroyed under the dominance of regressive and reactionary neoliberal institutions, ideolo-gies, values, and social relations. Market fundamentalism is inescapably the driving force of our time. A case in point: the total cost for the 2012 presidential campaign was $6 bil-lion, making clear not only that the U.S. political system has been corrupted by big money, but that American dem-ocratic values have been insidiously usurped by a mode of casino capitalism in which "the belief in free and unfettered markets has brought the world to the brink of ruin."[60] And this unimpeded and increasingly ubiquitous market culture is systematically destroying the formative conditions, rule of law, economic institutions, public spheres, and governing structures necessary for democracy to survive. Another dire effect, as Bauman observes, is that "visions have nowadays fallen into disrepute and we tend to be proud of what we should be ashamed of."[61]

America indeed seems inured to the ongoing threat of ecological destabilization produced by climate change and indifferent to the plight of those populations who suf-fer first and foremost from catastrophic events—natural and human—ranging from massive inequality and poverty to droughts, floods, super-storms, and increased extinction of species all around the planet. But new visions are arising among people across the United States and around the globe who refuse to equate capitalism with democracy or to accept a future shaped by the authoritarian dictates of a neoliberal society.[62] America needs a new language for politics, justice, compassion, and the obligations and entitlements of citizenship. The proactive powers of citizenship should not be reduced to the passive Coke-or-Pepsi choices of consumerism; a democratic society should not collapse into the image of the market; and human beings should not be dehumanized and reduced to disposable waste. Teddy Cruz is right in arguing that "democracy is not simply the right to be left alone. Rather it is defined by the coexistence with others in space, a collective ethos, regardless of social media, that unconditionally stands for [economic, political, and] social rights."[63] A democracy can only fulfill its promise when it safeguards all of its citizens. As Bauman argues, "society can only be raised to the level of community as long as it effectively protects its members against the horrors of misery and indignity; that is, against the terrors of being excluded [and] being condemned to 'social redundancy' and otherwise consigned to [being] 'human waste.'"[64]

Alain Badiou has argued that progressives should not trap themselves in a crisis of negation, one that rules out the possibility of struggle, resistance, and emancipatory change.[65] He suggests there is a need not only to challenge the corrupt and moribund version of democracy that now dominates the United States, but also to imagine what kind of institutions, culture, power relations, and modes of governance are possible. At stake here is not just the urgency to develop an enlightened civic imagination that embraces the moral concepts of conscience, decency, self-respect, and human dignity, but also a notion of collective struggle that fights for the social foundations that makes these concepts and public policy meaningful. In part, this can only happen when humanity frees itself from the authoritarian ideologies that attempt to either commercialize, criminalize, or simply abandon people, families, and whole communities.[66] Employing a language of both critique and hope helps create solidarities against such dehumanization; it unites contemporary struggles with the challenge of producing a new political vocabulary and approach to the future that refuses to mimic the present.

Radical civic imagination, political will, and democratic politics and pedagogy can be seen in full bloom in the contemporary abolition movement, post-Occupy networks, Strike Debt, and other insurgent and progressive social movements. It increasingly appears a range of existing crises have opened up new opportunities for critique, collective struggle, and hope—counterforces to the new authoritarianism and the violence of organized forgetting. A collective political gaze that envisions new socio-economic relations may soon energize civic culture, reshape democratic public spheres, and create new interfaces with a variety of individuals, groups, and publics. As Naomi Klein has pointed out, rather than use disasters as right-wing conservatives do—to further remove those marginalized by race, age, and class from economic resources, political privileges, and ethical considerations—many young people are engaging in the necessary but slow work of developing new modes of critical education, horizontally controlled and responsible cultural apparatuses, and social movements that would make true democracy possible.[67] Central to such efforts is a collective sense of urgency, agency, and vision that prompts new ways of thinking and acting within new civic spaces and public spheres. Klein's call for using moments of crisis to broaden the democratic space is a noble one, yet action needs to be spurred not only by the shock waves of natural disasters but also by the hidden and ongoing crisis of disposability that spreads the poison of dehumanization throughout American culture and society.

The late Tony Judt wanted to re-open a conversation about politics, the language of justice, popular rights, and the possibility of public action. Judt feared that the most dangerous threat America now faces is a corrosive "loss of conviction, a loss of faith in the culture of open democracy, a sense of skepticism and withdrawal which is probably already quite far advanced."[68] He argued that

> laudable goals—fighting climate change, opposing war, advocating public healthcare or penalizing bankers—are united by nothing more than the expression of emotion. In our political as in our economic lives, we have become consumers: choosing from a broad gamut of competing objec-

tives, we find it hard to imagine ways or reasons to combine these into a coherent whole. We must do better than this.[69]

Judt's comments are particularly appropriate in the aftermath of Hurricane Sandy. His was a call to move beyond single-issue movements in order to address and interconnect multiple struggles into "a conversation about society at large."[70] He rightly argued that what has "been lacking for social movements [is the need] to find a common ground beyond the fragmentation of particularized politics, to address the totality of systems steeped in authoritarian practices."[71]

Dorothy Roberts adds to the urgency of the demand for broad-based social movements in her brilliant book *Fatal Intervention*, in which she calls for "recognizing the relationship between neoliberalism, state authoritarianism . . . and a corporatized definition of citizenship that endangers the democratic freedoms of all Americans."[72] For Roberts any viable notion of politics demands both a discourse of critique and possibility, one that is essential for challenging "aggressive state surveillance, extreme human deprivation, and unspeakable brutality against whole populations on the basis of race."[73] She further elaborates insisting that "choosing the path for a common humanity and social change" demand a new understanding of politics that

> creates the potential for alliances among groups that see the dangerous potential in the escalating march from state support for public welfare toward

market-based solutions and repression of people
who are suffering most from this trend. Antiracist,
disability rights, and economic, gender, reproductive, and environmental justice movements all have
a stake in [creating] coalitions [that] provide hope
for broad-based social movements . . . in favor of
the radical restructuring of our society in to one
that respects the humanity of all people.[74]

The physical and political wreckage produced by Hurricane Sandy and the ideological machinery of disposability witnessed in its wake can only be understood within
this broader view of politics and society. Hurricane Sandy
should remind Americans that they have to be vigilant about
what populations are considered disposable and whose lives
are considered "unreal . . . neither alive nor dead, but inter-
minably spectral."[75] The shameful response to Sandy should
prompt the American public to be more than emotionally
moved in moments of future crisis: it should urge people
to become responsible here and now for what is happening within a larger constellation of political, historical, economic, and cultural forces. We cannot collectively afford to
ignore the pattern of warning signs. To do so will render not
only an increasing number of individuals and groups disposable, but also the very promise of democracy unintelligible
and cast outside of the realm of reason, hope, and struggle.

FOUR

THE VANISHING POINT OF U.S. DEMOCRACY

There's nothing that scares the rulers of America more than the prospect of democracy breaking out.
—David Graeber

We live at a time when the charged political rhetoric of "enemies," "terrorists," and "militants" is used by the United States as a justification not only for killing people suspected of wrongdoing but also the unfortunate innocent people who happen to be near them when U.S. attacks are executed. Normalizing the notion of permanent war and assigning Orwellian labels to acts of state violence and aggression have made it easier for the United States to carry out heinous acts both internally and internationally. For example, the U.S. has kidnapped people suspected of offenses, held them in CIA "black sites," and subjected them to extraordinary rendition—"the practice [of] taking detainees to and from U.S. custody without a legal process" and "handing [them] over to countries that practiced torture."[1] As a 2013 report from the Open Society Foundation points out, since 9/11 the CIA has illegally kidnapped and tortured over 136 people and has been aided in its abhorrent endeavours by 54 other countries.[2] All of this was done in secrecy, and when it was eventually exposed the Obama administration refused to press criminal charges against those government officials who committed atrocious human rights abuses, thereby signalling to the military and various intelligence agencies that they would not be held accountable for engaging in such egregious and illegal violations. In the United States, the principle that torture, kidnapping, and the killing of both noncitizens and citizens without due process is actually a prohibited and illegitimate use of state power has been slowly dismantled—perhaps even suffering the fate of the Geneva Conventions, which appear increasingly to be perceived as too quaint to be operative.

Excessive torture, cruel and unusual punishment, secret detention, and the violation of civil liberties are undeniably features of current government policy. They are also deeply engrained in American history and have become increasingly normalized in popular culture. For example, commercial representations of torture appear in a variety of entertainment products ranging from the infamous former television series *24* to the highly acclaimed Hollywood film, *Zero Dark Thirty*.[3] Whereas popular accounts of torture and other legal illegalities prior to 2001 were viewed largely as the acts of desperate and psychologically unbalanced individuals or rogue governments, the post-9/11 climate has accommodated such representations, as torture has become common fare in mainstream culture—from action films and TV dramas to comedies. As torture moves from state policy to screen culture, it contains "an echo of the pornographic in maximizing the pleasure of violence."[4] In this instance, the spectacle of violence mimics a new kind of obscenity that has engulfed American society, from children's cartoons and gory video games to adult entertainment. Torture is now a mainstay of what might be called the state-sanctioned carnival of cruelty designed to delight and exhilarate, while in real-life torture has been shamelessly accepted, like weapons of mass destruction and capital punishment, as ironically necessary for "security." In both politics and popular culture, torture, violence, and the culture of cruelty have been further separated from considerations of ethics, jurisprudence, accountability, and human rights.[5]

This retreat from moral responsibility reveals more than political failure, and more than a perverse victory for those who argue for the acceptability of what was once considered unthinkable in a civilian democracy. It signals the dismantling of a politics in which matters of power, justice, governance, and social responsibility are inextricably connected to democratic institutions, laws, values, and education. This is the emergence of a kind of antipolitics in which the obligations of justice and responsibility to others have been overtaken by a propaganda of fear, an increasingly corporatized national security agenda, and a war without end that has turned Americans into the accomplices of a tyrannical and terrorist state apparatus. Under such circumstances, the critical project of democracy, if not citizenship itself, is replaced by enforced quietism, obedience, and a state of emergency that "eradicates political freedom, democratic processes, and legality as such."[6]

The rise of an authoritarian and militaristic surveillance state—one marked by its flight from moral and political responsibility—has been made more acceptable by a widespread willingness to overlook, if not celebrate, the ongoing violation of civil liberties as a central theme of government policy, military conduct, the news media, and popular culture in general. Mainstream culture is flooded with endless representations of rogue individuals, government officials, and the police operating outside of the law as a legitimate way to seek revenge, implement vigilante justice, and unscrupulously violate human rights and civic duty. TV programs such as *Dexter* and *Person of Interest* as well as a spate of Hollywood films such as *Gangster Squad* and *Django Unchained* have provided spectacles of legal lawlessness and violence unchecked by ethical considerations and allegedly justified by the pursuit of noble ends.

The culture of ambient violence, manufactured fear, and invasive surveillance takes a toll politically and ethically on any democratic society, especially when challenging them is portrayed as a suspicious, unpatriotic, gateway behavior that could lead to serious crime in the same way that sipping beer might eventually lead to injecting heroin. Unfortunately, the line between fiction and material reality has blurred, and it has become more difficult to determine one from the other. Not only on the screen, but also within the hallowed spheres of politics and governance, forms of violence and violations of civil rights that should be unthinkable in a democracy are now lauded as effective tactics in the war on terrorism, and are rarely subjected to critical scrutiny. One of the more notable cases of this newfound toleration of human rights abuses is former vice president Dick Cheney's infamous statement to Tim Russert on NBC's *Meet the Press* in which he commented that the Bush administration would have to "work . . . the dark side." There is also the 2006 declaration by John Brennan in which he stated that the United States has "to take off the gloves" in some areas in order to wage a war against terrorism. And while torture has been denounced by President Obama, his administration has in actuality created a new foundation for violating civil rights and transgressing the law.

As the white paper memo released in winter 2013 by the Justice Department's Office of Legal Counsel makes clear, Obama has put into play government policies so extreme and brutal that the administration has propelled itself to the vanishing point of acceptable illegalities. This is evident in the administration's claim, duly noted even in the mainstream press, that it can target and kill American citizens anywhere on the globe.[7] The emergence of such practices has little to do with a reasonable need to promote national security or a country acting in self defense. On the contrary, such policies represent America's slide into barbarism, made all too vivid by the fact that the officials who are responsible for them are not held accountable, but are instead elevated to the highest positions in the American government. Witness the nomination of John Brennan as the next director of the CIA. Moreover, the Obama administration has now carried the institutionalization of pathological violence to an extreme with the assertion that a few officials in the highest reaches of government can decide which Americans and foreigners can be targeted and killed as enemies of the United States.

The release of the Justice Department's white paper, the confirmation hearings for John Brennan as the next CIA director, and the publication of *Globalizing Torture: CIA Secret Detention and Extraordinary Rendition* all provide stark evidence of the seamless assault on American democracy under both Republican and Democrat administrations.[8] These indices reveal, in turn, a society in which terror becomes as totalizing as the loss of any sense of ethical and political responsibility.

A critical perspective must take into account more than revelations that the United States is losing its moral compass or is violating civil liberties and promoting human rights abuses, though these troubling matters should not be dismissed. What mainstream commentary seems to miss is the degree to which the United States has come to exercise scorn toward democracy itself, such that it now openly spies on and invades the privacy of virtually the entire population. The white paper, furthermore, reveals a mode of governance, policy, and practice that is deeply antidemocratic in its claim to be able to use lethal, yet legal, force against U.S. citizens anywhere on the globe. When secrecy replaces judicial review and presidential power can be invoked without limits to kill Americans, it becomes difficult to recognize the United States as a democratic civilian nation. Marshaling an inverted version of legality reminiscent of Orwell's *1984* to authorize the claim that Americans can be killed without due process, the white paper justifies assassinating American citizens if they are a "senior operational leader of al-Qa'ida or associated force," if they "pose an imminent threat of violent attack to the United States," and if their "capture is infeasible."[9] This tactical distortion of language operates in the dead zone of morality, reason, and jurisprudence. More-over, the justification for such actions becomes meaningless in light of the administration's claim that its decisions require no external authorization or review—what it does can be done in secret, hidden from the public domain, and it need not provide evidence to a judge before or after an attack.[10] What is truly shocking is that an American citizen can be targeted for assassination by the U.S. government without the latter having to provide any proof of guilt—or the former being given an opportunity to establish innocence. This is more than a desecration of due process or a violation of constitutional and human rights: it is the open manifestation of authoritarianism. Glenn Greenwald captures this in his insightful comments:

> The most extremist power any political leader can assert is the power to target his own citizens for execution without any charges or due process, far from any battlefield. The Obama administration has not only asserted exactly that power in theory, but has exercised it in practice. . . . The definition of an extreme authoritarian is one who is willing blindly to assume that government accusations are true without any evidence presented or opportuni-

ty to contest those accusations. This memo—and the entire theory justifying Obama's kill list—centrally relies on this authoritarian conflation of government accusations and valid proof of guilt. They are not the same and never have been. Political leaders who decree guilt in secret and with no oversight inevitably succumb to error and/or abuse of power. Such unchecked accusatory decrees are inherently untrustworthy . . . that's why due process is guaranteed in the Constitution and why judicial review of government accusations has been a staple of western justice since the Magna Carta: because leaders can't be trusted to decree guilt and punish citizens without evidence and an adversarial process. That is the age-old basic right on which this memo, and the Obama presidency, is waging war.[11]

The administration's legal rhetoric and the practices it legitimates increasingly make the United States look like the ruthless Latin American dictatorships that seized power in the 1970s in part by appealing to paranoia, fear, insecurity, and the use of extralegal practices to defend barbaric acts of assassinations, torture, abuse, and disappearance. The writer Isabel Hilton rightly invokes this repressed piece of history and what it reveals about the current Obama administration. She writes:

The delusion that office holders know better than

the law is an occupational hazard of the powerful and one to which those of an imperial cast of
mind are especially prone. Checks and balances—
the constitutional underpinning of the democratic
idea that no one individual can be trusted with un-
limited power—are there to keep such delusions
under control. . . . When disappearance became
state practice across Latin America in the 70s it
aroused revulsion in democratic countries where
it is a fundamental tenet of legitimate government
that no state actor may detain—or kill—another
human being without having to answer to the law.[12]

Not only has the Obama administration discarded the
principles of justice, judicial review, and international law
in asserting its right to kill Americans without any limits imposed on its authority, it openly flaunts such behavior as integral to how the United States defines itself in
a post-9/11 world. And while it has agreed to release its
legal reasoning for killing U.S. citizens by armed drones,
it appears to have done so only "to ease pressure on John
Brennan, the architect of the drone strategy, at his Sen-
ate confirmation hearing as CIA Director."[13] How can any
American possibly talk about living in a democracy when
the president of the United States claims that he and a few
high-ranking government officials have the right and "the
power . . . to carry out the targeted killing of American
citizens who are located far away from any battlefield, even
when they have not been charged with a crime, even when

they do not present any imminent threat in any ordinary meaning of that word"?[14]

In a genuine democracy, citizens exercise their constitutionally protected powers, checks and balances limit unaccountable authority, and human rights are upheld rather than scorned. The task of governance and leadership is not to promote dangerous policies, but to draw out injustices embedded in the recesses of the past and the present, to make clear that the cover of secrecy and silence will not protect those who violate the law, and to reject forms of patriotic militarism that sanction illegality in the name of a permanent war on terrorism. There is more needed here than a call for transparency and the rejection of a government that imprisons and eavesdrops on U.S. citizens—or kills them without charges, trial, and due process. There is a crucial obligation on the part of democratic leadership and governance to uphold some measure of accountability and to redress policies and practices that implicate the United States in a long history of torture, one extending from the genocide of Native Americans to the enslavement of millions of Africans and their descendants to the killing of 21,000 Vietnamese under the aegis of the CIA's infamous Phoenix Program. The purpose of remembering this history is not to induce shame, but to recognize that such atrocities were normalized by political conditions and institutionalized policies that must be excised from American domestic and foreign policies if there is to be hope for a future that does not simply repeat the past.

What is missing in the refusal to make visible the U.S.

government's reorganization into an authoritarian surveillance state is the necessity for the American people to see what is wrong with such actions, who should be held accountable, why such invasive and cruel acts should not happen again, and what actions must be taken to open up the possibilities for society to exercise collective judgments that enable a rejection of past actions as well as the possibility of a more just future. Moreover, as Maria Pia Lara argues, refusing to narrate human cruelty is tantamount to relinquishing the moral imperative to build a transformed democratic community. She contends that exposing and engaging the hidden dimensions of cruelty and abuses of human rights is part of accepting a moral responsibility "directed at making others understand that what happened did not need to happen." Such narratives provide "a moral sense of the need to keep examining the past in order to . . . build a space for self-reflection [and] define the process of establishing a connection between the collective critical examination of past catastrophes and the learning processes in which societies engage."[15]

At a time in history when American society is facing the quasi-militarization of everyday life and endlessly exposed to mass-produced spectacles of commodified and ritualized violence, a culture of cruelty has become deeply entrenched and more easily tolerated. Beyond creating a moral and affective void in the collective consciousness—a refusal to recognize and rectify the illegal and morally repugnant violence, abuse, and suffering imposed on those alleged to be dangerous and disposable others—such a culture contributes to the undoing of the very fabric of civilization and justice. The descent into barbarism can take many forms, but one version may be glimpsed when torture becomes a defining feature of what a country considers acceptable policy (to say nothing of commercial entertainment), or the majority of its inhabitants remains passive when the president asserts the right to put together a kill list in order to execute American citizens without any form of civilian judicial process or review. How else to explain the fact that 49 percent of the American public "consider torture justified at least some of the time" and a full 71 percent "refuse to rule it out entirely"?[16]

Frank Rich has suggested that the American public's indifference to national security issues is partly due to the massive hardships and suffering many Americans have endured as a result of the Great Recession.[17] This may be true, but what this perspective overlooks are the ever-growing authoritarian forces now suppressing the advance of civilian-centered democracy. The civic imagination is in retreat in American society, and the public spheres that make it possible are under direct assault. As Morris Berman reminds us, "there is no real meaning in the corporate-consumer state, which is at once empty and idiotic."[18] This loss of meaning is matched by a loss of social conscience, resulting in a kind of commercialized insularity that erects firewalls against acknowledging the realities of widespread impoverishment and possibilities of human compassion and community.[19] How else to explain the liberal and conservative responses to Obama's kill list and targeting of American citizens in which the only issue at stake seems to be the lack of oversight for such killings?[20] How else to explain public inaction about the everyday violence of poverty, a state of misery to which at least one in every six people in the U.S. currently wallow? Surely, public paralysis in regard to these and other correctable injustices are characteristic of populations subjected to the warfare mentalities perpetrated by deeply authoritarian regimes.

Many elements of American political and popular culture are in dire need of being condemned, unlearned, and transformed through modes of critical education and public debate if civilian democracy is to survive as more than a distant and unfulfilled promise. Americans have lived too long with governments that use power to promote violent acts, conveniently hiding their guilt behind secrecy and silence while selectively punishing those considered expendable—in prisons, public schools, foster care institutions, and urban slums. As Tom Engelhardt points out, what has not sunk in for most Americans, including those voices in the mainstream media, is that the United States has become a lockdown state—or more appropriately an authoritarian state—made evident by the fact that U.S. authorities can:

> torture at will; imprison at will, indefinitely and without trial; assassinate at will (including American citizens); kidnap at will anywhere in the world and 'render' the captive in the hands of allied torturers; turn any mundane government document (at least 92 million of them in 2011 alone) into a classified object and so help spread a penumbra of

secrecy over the workings of the American government; surveil Americans in ways never before attempted (and only 'legalized' by Congress after the fact, the way you might back date a check); make war perpetually on their own say-so; and transform whistleblowing—that is, revealing anything about the inner workings of the lockdown state to other Americans—into the only prosecutable crime that anyone in the complex can commit.[21]

Such policies point to more than ethically bereft and atrophied modes of governance, politics, and culture: they point inexorably to the dark caverns of a society that has embraced the foundations of authoritarianism.

Democracy has been hijacked in the United States by right-wing extremism, corporate power, the military-industrial-academic complex, and a demagogic cultural apparatus—together working to create a state of emergency that nevertheless appears to "lack the kind of collective sense of urgency that would prompt us to fundamentally question our own ways of thinking and acting, and form new spaces of operation."[22] The consolidation of an authoritarian state reaches a fateful tipping point when the government engages in killing its own citizens anywhere in the world without facing any resistance on a moral level, let alone a legal one. All of us are now potential targets and within easy shooting range of the U.S. surveillance state.

FIVE

LOCKDOWN USA: LESSONS FROM THE BOSTON MANHUNT

A tragedy of errors: nobody knows any more who is who.
The smoke of the explosions forms part of the much larger
curtain of smoke that prevents all of us from seeing clearly.
From revenge to revenge, terrorism obliges us to walk to
our graves. I saw a photo, recently published, of graffiti on
a wall in NYC: "An eye for an eye makes the whole world
blind."[1]

—Eduardo Galeano

The American public rightfully expressed a collective sigh of relief and gratitude toward law enforcement authorities when the manhunt for the Boston Marathon bombers came to an end. The trauma and anxiety felt by the people of Boston and to some degree by the larger society over the heinous attacks on civilians were no doubt heightened given the legacy of 9/11. Since the tragic events of September 11, 2001, the nation has been subjected to "a media spectacle of fear and unreason delivered via TV, news sites, and other social media."[2] It has also been engulfed in nationwide hysteria over Muslim militants, insurgents, and terrorists. Perhaps to an extent greater than any previous historical moment, the American public has been immersed in a manipulative culture of fear and aggression shaped by a law-and-order mentality that promises personal safety, certainty, and collective protection. The constant marketing of "security" has amounted to a Faustian bargain in which Americans have traded their constitutional rights and powerful civil liberties for the increasingly invasive presence of a militarized surveillance state run by armed authorities who show little regard for human rights, justice, or democracy. The dystopic possibility of a society increasingly monitored, deterred, and coerced by an Orwellian national security complex has now become a reality. The United States of Fear has now merged with the United States of Amnesia as news of secret armies and wars along with clandestine assassinations, illegal legalities, and unprecedented state-sanctioned surveillance barely get a yawn from the American public.

The collective expressions of relief, compassion, and appreciation were reasonable and appropriate once the threat from the Boston Marathon bombers had ended. But such feelings can only be short-lived in a country that is losing its capacity to question itself, and instead embraces a mode of historical amnesia "in which forgetting has become more important than learning."[3] In the aftermath of such a tragedy, what was needed was thoughtful analysis about the significance of locking down an entire city and what such actions might mean, not simply for the present or the future of urban living but for democracy itself. The decision to lock down Boston was generally left unquestioned by the mainstream media, though a number of progressive and left-leaning intellectuals raised serious questions about the use and implications of the measure, particularly with respect to the abridging of civil liberties, the squelching of dissent, and the legitimation of the spectacle of the war machine. For example, Michael Schwalbe argued that he was troubled by what the lockdown foreshadows, with its connotation of authoritarian control, its increasing use in different contexts, and its ongoing normalization in American society. He wrote:

> When I hear that authorities have locked down a school, a workplace, a transit system, a cell phone network, or a city, the subtext seems unmistakable: We are now in control. Listen carefully and do as you are told. What I hear is the warden saying that communication will flow in one direction only, and that silence and obedience are the only options.[4]

Other commentators suggested the lockdown represented a massive overreaction that was symptomatic of a larger social crisis. Steven Rosenfeld argued that "beyond lingering questions of whether the government went too far by shutting down an entire city and whether that might encourage future terrorism, a deeper and darker question remains: why is America's obsession with evil so selective?"[5] This was an important point, and it was largely ignored in most commentary on the tragedy. Implicit in Rosenfeld's question is why the notion of security is limited to concerns over personal safety and the fear of attacks by terrorists, rather than the imminent dangers posed by predatory corporate enrichment practices, the shredding of the safety net for millions of Americans, the imprisonment of one out of every hundred Americans, or the transformation of public schools into adjuncts of the punishing and surveillance state?

Lockdown as a policy and mode of control distorts the notion of security by mobilizing fear and leaving the public no option other than to trade civil liberties for increased militarized security. The lockdown that took place in Boston serves as a reminder of how narrow the notion of security has become in that it is almost entirely associated with personal safety, but never with nationwide insecurities stemming from community impoverishment and environmental abuse, a lack of social provisions and health care, and the use of mass incarceration as a response to chronic social injustices. Increasingly, lockdown serves as a metaphor for how America responds to issues facing a range of institutions, including immigration detention centers, schools, hospitals, public housing, and prisons. Lockdown is the new common sense of a militarized society and underlies the proliferation of zones of unchecked state surveillance, policing, and brutality inflicted on the citizenry. Some have argued that because the people of Boston were only advised to stay inside while police in paramilitary formation flooded the city, it is not accurate to suggest there was a lockdown. But the real concern here should have focused on what it means when the militarized security state is out in full force in a particular city and it is no longer necessary for it to impose martial law in order to do so. Rather than follow formal procedure, all that is necessary is for the national security state to give "advice" and thereby legitimate a military occupation regardless of legal processes, let alone consent.[6]

Security in this instance is linked to a hyper-individualistic society that "reveres competitiveness and celebrates unrestrained individual responsibility, with an antipathy to anything collective that might impede market forces"—a world in which the Darwinian survival-of-the-fittest ethos rules and the only values that matter are exchange values.[7] In this panopticon-like social order, there is little support for society being structured and governed in the public interest, of the importance of sustaining public necessities such as decent housing, job programs for the under employed, housing, health care, parks, libraries, community media, and universal education for everyone. Sustained fear becomes an excuse for policies that inflict cruelty upon society's most vulnerable people. Yet, as David Oshinsky writes, a "nation's legitimate concern for security in uncertain times" is no excuse for turning such a fear "into something partisan, repressive, and cruel."[8]

In a society in which any critical analysis of the forces that precipitate violent attacks of this nature is immediately condemned and stigmatized as outrageous if not suspicious activity, there is a stultifying logic that regards contextualizing an event as tantamount to justifying it. This crippling impediment to public dialogue may be why the militarized response to the Boston Marathon bombings, infused with the fantasy of the "homeland" as a battlefield and the idealization of the paramilitarized surveillance state, was for the most part given a pass in mainstream media. Of course, there is more at stake here than misplaced priorities and the dark cloud of historical amnesia and anti-intellectualism, there is also the drift of American society into a media-enforced authoritarianism in which boots on the ground and the securitization of everyday life serve as a source of pride and entertainment—or, for many disposable groups, a source of terror.

In the immediate aftermath of the marathon bombing, it may have been the case that shock and collective dislocation left little room to think about the context in which the bombing took place or the implications of a lockdown strategy that hint at the broader danger of exchanging security for freedom, especially given the general lockdown of the country since 9/11. Yet any subsequent attempt to suggest that the overly militarized response to the bombings was less about protecting people than legitimating the ever-expanding reach of military operations to solve domestic problems was met with either disdain or silence in the dominant media. In the midst of the emotional fervor that followed the bloody Boston marathon bombings, various pundits decried any talk about a possible overreaction to the event and that such measures gave tacit approval to a police state. One commentator, in a moment of emotive local hysteria, referred to such critics as "outrage junkies" and claimed they were "masturbating in public," then insisted he was washing his hands of what he termed "bad rubbish."[9] This particular line of thought with its discursive infantilism and echoes of nationalistic jingoism ominously suggested that what happened in Boston should only register as a deeply felt emotional event, one that was desecrated by trying to understand it within a broader historical and political context. Perhaps even more disturbing than the political offensive leveled against such critics was the intensity of right-wing diatribes that used the Boston Marathon bombing as an excuse to further the expansion of the surveillance state with its increasingly invasive mechanisms of weaponization, social control, and secrecy, and its exercise of soft forms of martial law. And equally repulsive was how the Boston bombing produced an ample amount of nativist paranoia about immigrants and the quest for an "enemy combatant" behind every door.

Another indicator of bad faith was evident in the comments of right-wing pundits, broadcasting elites, and squeamish liberals who amped up the frenzied media spectacle surrounding the Boston Marathon bombings. Many of them suggested, without apology, that the country should be grateful for an increase in invasive searches, the suspension of constitutional protections, the embrace of total surveillance, and the ongoing normalization of the security state and Islamophobia.[10] For example, Republican senator Chuck Grassley of Iowa referred to the attacks in an effort to undo immigration reform, no longer concealing his disdain for immigrants, especially people who practice Islam and people from Mexico.[11] And Republican representative Peter King of New York reasserted his long standing racism by repeatedly arguing that the greatest threat of terrorism faced by the United States "is coming from the Muslim community" and that it might be time for state and federal authorities to spy on all Muslims.[12] According to King, "police have to be in the community, they have to build up as many sources as they can, and they have to realize that the threat is coming from the Muslim community and increase surveillance there," and "we can't be bound by political correctness."[13] King seems to think that dismissing the rhetoric of political correctness provides a rationale for translating into policy his virulent Islamophobia and the national hallucination it feeds. Of course, King and others are simply channeling the racism of the cartoonish Ann Coulter who actually suggested that all "unauthorized immigrants in the United States might be terrorists."[14] This nativist paranoia is not new and has a long and disgraceful legacy in American history.

Further frightening offshoots of the bombings were the authoritarian tirades unleashed by several government officials that indicated how close dissent is to being treated as a crime, and how under siege public space is by the forces of manufactured terrorism. Republican senator Lindsey Graham of South Carolina argued that President Obama should not only deny Dzhokhar Tsarnaev his constitutional rights by refusing to give him his Miranda warning, but also hold him as "an enemy combatant for intelligence gathering purposes."[15] As one commentator pointed out: "This is pretty breathtaking. Graham is suggesting that an American citizen, captured on American soil, should be deprived of basic constitutional rights."[16] Sadly, Graham is simply arguing for what many Americans have experienced since the tragic attack of September 11, 2001. The boundary between the military and civilian life has been dismantled, just as the boundaries between the "innocent and guilty, between suspects and non-suspects" have become increasingly blurred.[17] The international claim of solidarity that took place in the aftermath of 9/11, in which a number of countries insisted that "we are all Americans," has given way in American society to the zombie-like notion that "we are all suspects." There is more at stake here than hyped-up security or the rise of the surveillance state: there is a militarizing logic of war and authoritarianism that could very well translate into the death of democracy and the public sphere.

What is new in the current historical moment is how easily nativist paranoia and a culture of cruelty have become normalized, generating a public lexicon that appears to prefer state terrorism and authoritarianism over free and open democracy. For instance, New York State senator Greg Ball, channeling fellow Republican Dick Cheney, took this logic of state terrorism to its inevitable end point—reminding Americans of the degree to which the United States has lost its moral compass—when he posted a message from his Twitter account stating that the authorities should torture Tsarnaev. As Ball put it, "So, scum bag #2 in custody. Who wouldn't use torture on this punk to save more lives?"[18] There is more at work here than an evasion of ethical principle, to say nothing of international law. There is an erasure of the very notion of a sovereign and democratic polity, along with a frightening collective embrace of a dehumanizing authoritarianism that indicate the near death of democracy in the United States.

Such unconsidered remarks should compel us to examine the state's use of lockdown procedures within the broader context of a savage market-driven society that sanctions a general culture of punishment and cruelty. This national drift toward increasing levels of acceptable violence is witnessed by the return of the nineteenth-century debtors' prisons in which people are jailed—and their lives ruined—for not being able to pay what amounts to trivial fines.[19] It is also evident in the attempts of some West Virginia Republican Party legislators to push for a policy that would force low-income school children to work in exchange for free lunches.[20] The flight from ethical responsibility associated with the rise of the punishing state and the politics of the lockdown can also be seen in the willingness of police forces around the country to push young children into the criminal justice system.[21] The increasing tendency in American politics, media, and entertainment to align with the forces of militarization, law enforcement measures, and the dictates of the national security state all contribute both to their normalization in everyday life and to an intolerance of protest and dissent.

The lockdown and ongoing search for those responsible for the Boston Marathon bombings were eminently political events because they amplified the already-in-place dreadful potential and real consequences of the never-ending war on terror and the antidemocratic processes it has produced at all levels of government, particularly an increasing diminishment of civil liberties. The post-9/11 script has become familiar and includes the authorized use of state-sponsored torture, the unchecked power of the president to conduct targeted assassinations, the use of warrantless searches, extraordinary renditions, secret courts, the constant monitoring of the entire population in pursuit of potential suspects, and a general chilling of free speech critical of state policy and power.[22] Another consequence of the war on terror is the increasing use of military drone strikes in Yemen and Pakistan, resulting in many innocent children and adults being killed. As Noam Chomsky points out, such attacks are "terrorizing villagers, turning them into enemies of the United States—something that years of jihadi propaganda had failed to accomplish. . . . There was no direct way to prevent the Boston murders. There are some easy ways to prevent likely future ones: by not inciting them."[23]

Since 9/11 we have witnessed the consolidation of a national surveillance state and the expansion of a lockdown mode of existence in a range of institutions that extends from schools and airports to the space of the city itself. Tom Engelhardt has argued that Dick Cheney, George W. Bush, and Donald Rumsfeld helped inaugurate the lockdown state after 9/11, and the price Americans have paid as a result far exceeds the threat of a terror attack.[24] The meaning of lockdown in this context has to be understood in broader terms as the use of military "solutions" to address problems for which such approaches are both unnecessary and further produce authoritarian and antidemocratic policies and practices. Under such circumstances, not only have civil liberties been violated in the name of national security, but the promise of national security has given rise to policies which are punitive, steeped in the logic of revenge, and support the rise of a punishing state whose echoes of authoritarianism are often lost in the paralysis of conscience that accompany the country's normalization of war, austerity and recession, and the militarization of everyday life.

Glenn Greenwald, while a columnist for *The Guardian*, similarly insists that the Boston Marathon bombing signified a political event because it "connects to larger questions about our culture and because it was infused with all kinds of political messages about Muslims, about radicalism, about what the proper role of the police and the military are in the United States."[25] But the few examples like this—offering critical analyses of the unnecessary imposition of a lockdown in Boston, especially Watertown—have typically missed the fact that the United States was essentially already in lockdown mode in a way that has been intensifying since 9/11. That is, a number of critics raised questions about the abridgement of civil rights and the specter of excessive policing after the marathon bombing, but they discussed these as one-off events; few have made the connection to the continuity and expansion of the logic of lockdown that even predates September 11, 2001, and which can be traced back to the disproportionate incarceration of people of color.[26] This longer history of the punishing state has been addressed by W. E. B. Du Bois, Angela Davis, Michelle Alexander, Ruth Wilson Gilmore, Douglas A. Blackmon, and others, and it need not be repeated here. What does need to be addressed is how the concept and tactics of the prison now shapes a whole range of institutions and antisocial sensibilities, making clear how the population United States is quietly accepting lockdown as yet another form of subordination to the authoritarian state. While the Boston lockdown involved issuing a "request" for the public to stay inside, it displayed all of the attributes of tyrannical rule, especially in Watertown where house-to-house searches effectively treated the residents as feared criminals.

Lockdown as a concept and strategy, therefore, gains its meaning and legitimacy under specific historical conditions informed by particular modes of ideology, governance, and policing. Lockdown cannot be understood outside of the euphemism of homeland security, and the view aptly expressed by Lindsey Graham, that the Boston Marathon bombing is "Exhibit A of why the homeland is the battlefield."[27] Graham's comments imply the dangerous correlate that everyone is a potential suspect and that domestic militarization and its embrace of perpetual war is a perfectly legitimate practice, however messy it might be when measured against principles of democracy, human rights, and the most basic tenets of constitutional law. At a time when the United States has embraced a number of antidemocratic practices extending from state torture to the ruthless militarized logic of a Darwinian politics of cruelty and disposability, the symbolic meaning of the lockdown is difficult to ignore, while its purpose has become indistinguishable from the authoritarian state that increasingly relies on it as a form of policing and disciplinary control. This becomes all the more obvious when comparing the lockdown in Boston to the response of other countries to terrorist acts. As Michael Cohen, a correspondent for *The Guardian*, points out:

The actions allegedly committed by the Boston marathon bomber, Dzhokhar Tsarnaev and his brother, Tamerlan, were heinous. [Three] people dead and more than [260 injured], some with shredded and amputated limbs. But Londoners, who endured IRA terror for years, might be forgiven for thinking that America over-reacted just a tad to the goings-on in Boston. They're right—and then some. What we saw was a collective freak-out like few that we've seen previously in the United States. It was yet another depressing reminder that more than 11 years after 9/11 Americans still allow themselves to be easily and willingly cowed by the "threat" of terrorism.[28]

Some would argue that locking down an entire city because a homicidal killer was on the loose can be attributed to how little experience Americans have with daily acts of terrorism—in contrast to Baghdad, Beirut, and other cities which are constantly subject to such attacks. While there is an element of truth to such arguments, what is missing from this position is a different and more frightening logic. Americans have become so indifferent to the militarization of everyday life that they barely blink when an entire city, school, prison, or campus is locked down. In fact, as part of the national indoctrination of lockdown, American school children are now subjected to lockdown drills, a normalization process which the *New York Times* describes as "the new fire drill."[29] In a society in which everyone is treated as a potential suspect or criminal "to be penalized, locked up or locked out," it is not surprising that institutions and policies are constructed that normalize a range of antidemocratic practices.[30] These include everything from invasive body searches by the police and the mass incarceration of people of color to the ongoing surveillance and securitization of schools, workplaces, social media, the Internet, businesses, neighborhoods, and individuals, all of which signify major government overreach that mimics the tactics of a police state.[31] At a time when prison, poverty, and a culture of cruelty and punishment inform each other and ensnare more and more Americans, the "governing-through-crime" complex moves across America like a fast-spreading virus.[32] In its wake, Mississippi schoolchildren are handcuffed for not wearing a belt or having the wrong color shoes;[33] young mothers who cannot pay a traffic ticket are sent to jail;[34] and, according to Michelle Alexander, "more African American men are in prison or jail, on probation or parole than were enslaved in 1850, before the Civil War began."[35]

These examples are not merely anecdotal. They point to the alarming degree to which lockdown has become a central tool and organizing logic in controlling those growing populations now considered disposable and subject to the machinery of social and civic death. The racist grammars of state violence that emerged during and after the lockdown of Boston speak to a connection between the violence of disposability that haunts American life and the state's increasing reliance on the use of force to implement and maintain its structures of inequality, abusive power, and domination.

Its ghostly presence spills over into Florida's "stand your ground" statute, stop-and-frisk policies, the militarization of local police forces, and the ever expanding presence of the carceral state. Within this system of coercion and control, matters of moral, social, and political responsibility are silenced in the name of security, even as efforts to pass legislation on gun control in order to prevent senseless violence and murder are routinely displaced by the assertion of individual rights. Americans rightly mourn the victims of the Boston bombings but are exposed to little about the ongoing killing of hundreds of children in the streets of Chicago. Nor is there a public outcry and mourning for the tragic deaths of over two hundred children killed as a result of drone attacks launched by the Obama administration inside Afghanistan and other countries. The term "evil," when deployed by the American media and its complicit politicians, becomes at once too broad and too narrow but insistently self-serving.[36] Evil is always lurking out there in some other place or person but never within those who seize upon the category to distance themselves from the atrocities with which they are directly complicit.[37]

Accordingly, the rush to lockdown must be understood within the wider political economy of the ongoing war on terror and the consolidation of the permanent warfare state, which now moves across and shapes a wide range of sites and institutions. Lockdown has been interwoven with militarized modes of governance, ideology, faith, and practice that categorize people in terms of being suspects, soldiers, enforcers, enemy combatants, criminals, clients, consumer pawns, or as being disposable: people with no money. Among the most severe implications is that the shift to permanent war forecloses the very possibility of judgment, informed argument and decision, and critical agency itself. Lockdown is complete public submission to absolute authority, and as such is intolerant of dissent. Its particular forms of social control are part of a long historical continuum that connects early-American systems of enslavement and human trafficking with today's systems of criminalization, incarceration, and still-practiced varieties of punishment considered to be acts of barbarity in many countries, including solitary confinement, torture, and human slaughter.

Public compliance with practices of lockdown increased following 9/11 with the normalization of constant war and the imposition of color-coded states of perpetual threat. Moreover, the values and actions that lockdown legitimates blur the lines between the wars at home and abroad, and between social investments and the ongoing financing of a culture of war and weaponization. The U.S. population is indoctrinated to serve the national security state, and "civic virtues such as freedom, equality, and citizenship are threaded into the militarized national narrative of conquest and conversion." If you see something, say something; otherwise remain silent.[38]

Tom Engelhardt has argued persuasively that the U.S. national security complex, with its "$75 billion or more budget," continues to expand and that "the Pentagon is, by now, a world unto itself, with a staggering budget at a moment when no other power or combination of powers comes near to challenging this country's might."[39] Moreover, under the guise of the war on terror, Republican and Democrat administrations have "lifted the executive branch right out of the universe of American legality. They liberated it to do more or less what it wished, as long as 'war,' 'terrorism,' or 'security' could be invoked. Meanwhile, with their Global War on Terror well launched and promoted as a multigenerational struggle, they made wartime their property for the long run."[40] Working in conjunction with state policy, lockdown culture further exalts military authority and thrives in a society that "can no longer even expect our public institutions to do anything meaningful to address meaningful problems."[41] One indication of the militarization of American society is the high social status now accorded to the military itself and the transformation of soldiers into uniformly heroic subjects and objects of national reverence.

As Michael Hardt and Antonio Negri point out:

What is most remarkable is not the growth in the number of soldiers in the United States but rather their social stature. . . . Military personnel in uniform are given priority boarding on commercial airlines, and it is not uncommon for strangers to stop and thank them for their service. In the United States, rising esteem for the military in uniform corresponds to the growing militarization of the society as a whole. All of this despite repeated revelations of the illegality and immorality of the military's own incarceration systems, from Guantánamo to Abu Ghraib, whose systematic practices border on if not actually constitute torture.[42]

At the same time, military values no longer operate within the exclusive realm and marginalized space of the armed forces or those governing structures dedicated to defense. On the contrary, the ideas, principles, and aggressive talk emerging from the national security sector shape the everyday lives of civilians, creating what Charles Derber and Yale Magrass call "a warrior society" and define as:

> culture and institutions which program civilians for violence at home as well as abroad. War celebrates the heroism of soldiers who use the same style weapons and ammunition used by the mass shooters at Newtown, Los Angeles, or Columbine. A warrior society values its armed forces as heroic protectors of freedom, sending a message that the use of guns [and the organized production of violence are] morally essential.[43]

Ulrich Beck is right in arguing that the "military is to democracy as fire is to water." He writes that military ideals reconceive people as machine-like bodies without minds:

> the life of a person is worth less than the lump of flesh in which he dwells. If democracy demands the individual's will, the military demands his subordination. If, in the former case, all power origi-

nates from the people, then, in the latter all orders come from above. . . . Wherever one looks, it is the same: democracy means openness, questioning, power-sharing, transparent decisions. Military is a synonym for secret, command, killing, strictly prohibited. There is no need to recite the rest.[44]

In America, militarism and mass surveillance are imposed and then euphemistically paraded as homeland security. This helps to explain a few things. First, it explains the public's silence in the face of not only the eradication and suppression of civil liberties, public values, and democratic institutions, but also the growing power of the financial elite and military-industrial-complex. Second, and relatedly, it explains the transformations of a number of institutions into militarized spheres more concerned about imposing punitive authority than creating the conditions for the production of an engaged and critical citizenry.

Within this context, lockdown signals nothing less than the open consolidation of a new kind of authoritarianism, and the beginning of an era in which democracy is replaced by increasingly invasive surveillance, weaponization, and intolerance of public dialogue, debate, dissent, transparency, and traditional forms of public accountability.

Authoritarianism and surveillance thrive on a culture of suspicion, intolerance, and media control. It abhors openness and dissent and flourishes in an ever-expanding web of subordination and secrecy. Federal and state authorities have used the cult of surveillance and the threat of punishment to deter whistleblowers and movement organizers, while at the same time allowing those who have committed acts of economic mass destruction and torture to go free. They deny requests from those who have been "interrogated" illegally who seek to take their case to the courts. In the name of "securing" the homeland, the rule of law disappears into the ever-expanding grid of surveillance, classified information, entrapment cases, cyberwarfare, targeted killings, and acts of aggression, sabotage, and abduction conducted by U.S. special operations forces. Tom Engelhardt rightly argues that America has become a country wedded to the self-deluding fantasy that the rule of law not only still prevails, but applies to everyone. He writes:

> What it means to be in such a post-legal world—to know that, no matter what acts a government official commits, he or she will never be brought to court or have a chance of being put in jail—has yet to fully sink in. . . . In reality, in the Bush and Obama years, the United States has become a nation not of laws but of legal memos, not of legality but of legalisms—and you don't have to be a lawyer to know it. The result? Secret armies, secret wars, secret surveillance, and spreading state secrecy, which meant a government of the bureaucrats about which the American people could know next to nothing. And it's all "legal."[45]

Pervasive secrecy in the age of the lockdown suggests

that the United States has more in common with authoritarian regimes than with flourishing democracies. The production of ignorance and secrecy are primary weapons of authoritarian governments that want to make state power invisible. An ignorant public constitutes one major quest of the security state, which refuses to be held accountable for its illegal and often murderous acts.[46] A glimpse of how state security views public awareness as a threat is evident in a statement expressed by the late Harvard political scientist Samuel P. Huntington. He writes: "The architects of power in the United States must create a force that can be felt but not seen. Power remains strong when it remains in the dark; exposed to the sunlight it begins to evaporate." [47] Yet the American people are still successfully persuaded to believe they live in a country that represents the apogee of freedom and democracy. As Brian Terrell argues, "prisons and the military, America's dominant institutions, exist not to bring healing to domestic ills or relief from foreign threats but to exacerbate and manipulate them for the profit of the wealthiest few, at great cost and peril for the rest of us."[48] Why aren't people pouring into the streets of American cities to protest the rise of the prison and military as America's dominant institutions?

What will it take for the American public to connect the increasing militarization of everyday life to the ways in which the prison-industrial complex destroys lives[49] and for-profit corporations have the power to put poor people in jails for being in debt?[50] Or, for that matter, to voice opposition to how school authorities punish young children by putting them in seclusion rooms,[51] while on a larger scale the U.S. government increasingly relies on solitary confinement in detaining immigrants?[52] When will the American people link images of the "shattered bodies, dismembered limbs, severed arteries . . . and terrified survivors" to the reports of over two hundred young children killed in Pakistan, Afghanistan, Yemen, and Somalia as a result of drone attacks launched by faux video gamers sitting in dark rooms in cities thousands of miles away from their targets?[53] In the face of the Boston Marathon bombings, the concern that haunts the American public should focus on much more than our capacity for compassion and solidarity in response to the victims of this tragedy: it should question how indifferent we have become to the conditions that only too readily have turned this terrible tragedy into just another exemplary register of the war on terror and a further legitimation for the military-industrial national security state.

Violence and its handmaidens—militarism and military culture—have become essential threads in the fabric of American life. We live in a culture in which a lack of imagination is matched by diminishing intellectual visions and a collective refusal to challenge injustices, however blatant and corrosive they may be. For instance, a political system completely corrupted by big money barely elicits, let alone sustains, any analysis and public outrage. [54] The mortgaging of the future for generations of young people for the profit of the few and other acts of mass economic predation do little to stir public indignation over the corruption inherent to the plutocratic political-economic system.[55] The embarrassing judgments of a judicial system that punishes impoverished people and allows the rich to go free in the face of crimes of economic mass destruction boggles the mind, but apparently not enough to stir widespread criticism. As Matt Taibbi says in *Rolling Stone*: "An arrestable class and an unarrestable class. We always suspected it, now it's admitted. So what do we do?"[56] The real challenge facing Americans is not achieving the illusory dream of winning the war on terror but finding a way to prevent authoritarian and predatory economic, political, and cultural forces that hold sway over American life from completely destroying civic society and any vestige of agency willing to oppose them.

Despite the violence of organized forgetting and the forces of structural repression and coercion, memory, imagination, and resistance endure. Today's generation of activists—especially those who drove the Occupy movement—demonstrate the existence of a massive civic subculture capable of mobilizing the political and moral courage necessary to challenge and defy authority while raising fundamental questions about the influence of the rich and the real social and ecological consequences of a market-based system.[57] Salman Rushdie has argued that political courage has become ambiguous and that the American public, among others across the globe, has "become suspicious of those who take a stand against the abuses of power or dogma," or even worse, blames them for upsetting people through their willingness to stand against and challenge orthodoxy or bigotry.[58] Gone, Rushdie argues, are the writers and intellectuals of the kind who opposed Stalinism, capitalist tyranny, and the various religious and ideological orthodoxies that seek to disengage thinking people and transform them into a silent and obedient underclass that complies with the ever-invasive dictates of power.

Of course, there continue to be examples of intellectuals, artists, educators, and ordinary people who do not tie their intellectual capital to the possibility of a summer cruise or the rewards provided to those who are silent in the face of injustice. Nor do they participate in Fox News–like platforms that seemingly offer instant celebrity status and substantial reward for demonstrating the pedagogical virtues of keeping the public politically illiterate while making it easier to push the informed and thoughtful to the margins of society. As Noam Chomsky has pointed out, these anti-public intellectuals are distinguishable by not only their "acceptance within the system of power and a ready path to privilege, but also the inestimable advantage of freedom from the onerous demands of thought, inquiry, and argument."[59]

In addition to considering public intellectuals and activists as inherently suspicious, U.S. surveillance culture powers a massive disimagination machine in which historical memory is hijacked as the struggles of the oppressed disappear, the "state as the guardian of the public interest is erased," and the expectation of institutions serving the public good evaporates.[60] At the same time, the imagination is usurped by inscriptions of violence that establish new patterns, such as a dangerous and hardened notion of masculinity in which men (and increasingly women) have to learn to be tough, deny vulnerability, punish and kill and experience it as pleasure, endure humiliation in the face of authority, and be willing to sacrifice limbs, mental stability, and life itself. In opposition to this culture and machinery of death, there is a need to reclaim the memories of diverse democratic movements in order to imagine a politics capable of resurrecting democratic institutions of governance, culture, and education. Moreover, the educative nature of politics has to be addressed in order to develop both new forms of individual and collective agency and vast social networks that can challenge the global concentration of economic and political power held by an ultra-small number of excessively wealthy individuals.

Gayatri Spivak has argued that "without a strong imagination, there can be no democratic judgment, which can imagine something other than one's own well-being."[61] The current historical conjuncture dominated by the discourse and institutions of neoliberalism and militarization present sa threat not just to the economy, but to the very possibility of imagining alternative ways of living, relating, communicating, and collectively getting things done. A generalized fear now shapes American society—one that thrives on insecurity, precarity, dread of punishment, and a perception of constant lurking threats. Any struggle that matters will have to reimagine and fight for a society in which it becomes possible once again to dream the project of a substantive democracy. This means, as Ulrich Beck has pointed out, looking for politics in new spaces and arenas outside of traditional elections, political parties, and "duly authorized agents."[62] It suggests developing public spaces outside of the regime of predatory corporatism and engaging in a type of counter politics that shapes society from the bottom up.

Central to such a challenge will be the educational task of inquiring not only how democracy has been lost under the current regime of neoliberal capitalism with its gangster rulers and production of organized irresponsibility and injustice, but also how the project of democracy can be retrieved through the joint power and efforts of workers, young people, educators, minorities, immigrants, activists, and others. At the present historical moment, lockdown culture is being disrupted in many societies. A fight for democracy is emerging across the globe and is being led by people who are unwilling to live in societies in which lockdown becomes further normalized as a tool for social control and repression. The future of democracy both in the United States and abroad rests precisely with those who are attempting to create new social movements built on a powerful vision of a democratic future and the durable organizations that will make it possible.

SIX

TEACHERS RESISTING NEOLIBERALISM AT HOME

Education is the most powerful weapon which you can use to change the world.

—Nelson Mandela

Across the globe, financial elites and authoritarian regimes are threatened by the transformative potential of civic democracy and are doing their best to counter the threat. Laying siege to the defining institutions of democracy, the ultra-wealthy are working relentlessly to increase the influence of money in politics and anything else that can be bought and bent to enrich them.[1] Hijacking "the affective and ideological spaces of neoliberalism," the rich and corporate elite have produced bleak emotional landscapes in which "the social damage wrought by deunionization, financialization and deeply embedded patterns of gender and racial discrimination are . . . disconnected from any wider social context."[2] Separating personal troubles from larger historical and political context, dominant social and political forces spin out of control as the tentacles of totalitarianism mangle the modern ideal of justice, equality, freedom, and democracy.[3] As Leo Gerard, president of the United Steelworkers writes, billionaire "vulture capitalists" like Tom Perkins are openly calling for increased security and power for the wealthy in the United States:

> Perkins contended *in a letter to the Wall Street Journal* that progressives and the 99 percent are persecuting America's wealthiest in the same way the Nazis murdered, raped and plundered the German Jewish minority during Kristallnacht. Then Perkins revealed his scheme to change the world, to crush the uppity 99 percent once and for all and make America what he would call a decent place for billionaires. It's simple. No more of that pesky one human, one vote. Perkins believes billionaires should get a vote for every dollar they pay in taxes.[4]

As market mentalities impose their influence on all aspects of society, democratic institutions and public spheres are being downsized, if they have not yet disappeared. As these institutions are dismantled—from public schools to health care centers—there is also a serious erosion of the discourses of community, justice, equality, public values, and the common good. One does not have to look too far into America's neoliberal educational culture to see how ruthlessly the inequality of wealth, income, and power bears down on those young people and brave teachers who are struggling every day to save the schools, unions, and modes of pedagogy that offer hope at a time when schools have become commercialized, students have been reduced to clients or disposable populations, and teachers and their unions have been increasingly demonized.

Chicago mayor Rahm Emanuel's decision to close down fifty public schools, mostly attended by children of color from low-income communities, is one more example of a savage system at work that uses the neoliberal politics of austerity and consolidation to further disenfranchise as many as 30,000 unskilled youth inhabiting the inner city. Of the fifty schools targeted to be closed, forty-nine serve elementary school children, "90 percent of whom are African American (in a district that is only 40 percent African American)."[5] The hidden agenda in this instance is not so invisible. Closing schools will result in massive layoffs and a weakening of the teachers' unions. It will free up land that can be gentrified to attract middle-class voters, and it will once again prove that poor minority students from communities of color, regardless of the hardships, if not danger, they face as a result of such closings are viewed as disposable—human waste to be relegated to the zones of terminal exclusion. Curtis Black has argued that over 3,900 homeless students will be impacted by the proposed mergers; given Chicago Public Schools' disastrous record in transitioning students to new schools, many students will be lost in the process.[6] Not only are teachers and parents concerned about displacing thousands of students to schools that do not offer any hope of educational improvement, they are also concerned about the safety of the displaced children, many of whom "will have to walk through violent neighborhoods, and go to school with other students who are considered enemies."[7]

Resistance to Emanuel's politics of closure and disposability is being challenged from a number of quarters, including from high school students themselves. Brian Sturgis, a Chicago high school senior and organizer with the group Chicago Students Organizing to Save Our Schools declared in an op-ed that Chicago students are prepared to fight for their schools. He writes:

> Mayor Emanuel and his Board of Education want to close 54 grammar schools around the city, all of which are in black and Latino communities: this is racist. These schools are also being judged based on assessments and tests given throughout the year: this is foolish. These school closings will leave neighborhoods dismantled, parents lost, students unaccounted for, and more importantly, will put children in harmful situations: this is dangerous.[8]

Sturgis is right in that such policies are not simply misguided: they are part of a racist script that makes clear that children of color are disposable and that their safety is irrelevant.[9] How else to explain the mayor's plan to produce "safe passage" for children who are crossing the city to get to their new school buildings by ordering firefighters to patrol the new routes, even though the firefighters have made it clear that they are not trained for this type of special duty?[10] Mayor Emanuel, along with his neoliberal allies in a number of cities such as Philadelphia, inhabit a dead zone of capitalism, a zone marked by an open refusal to serve all sectors of the public in a dignified and egalitarian manner. There is no other way to interpret the right-wing educational reform policy driving massive school closings in Philadelphia, New York City, Detroit, and other cities in which low-income and poor minority students are displaced, put at risk, and abandoned to the dictates of a neoliberal agenda—an agenda that aims to "create privately managed charter schools that are non-union schools."[11]

Emanuel's policies are likewise symptomatic of a larger war against teachers, public goods, and the social contract. We increasingly live in a culture that uses the vocabulary of "choice" and exhibits a denial of reality—a denial of massive inequality, social disparities, the irresponsible concentration of power in relatively few hands, and a growing machinery of social and civil death.[12] As power becomes global and is removed from local and nation-based politics, more and more individuals and groups have become imaginary others managed by the consequences of how a free-floating elite class reshapes society in their interests and erases those who in any way minimize their enrichment or inhibit its pursuit. Consequently, there are growing numbers of people whose hardship and suffering are simply ignored. Power has lost its moorings in democratic institutions and removes itself from any sense of social, civic, and political responsibilities. At the same time, the dead zone of capital accumulation and dispossession destroys those public spheres and collective structures such as public and higher education that are capable of resisting the deregulatory pressures of the pure market and the antidemocratic strictures it imposes on American society. Peter Brogan sums this up well in his analysis of the forces behind the current attacks on teachers and public education. He writes that the neoliberal agenda behind such attacks has

> been outlined in numerous planning documents from different city administrations, some of which have been drafted by the Commercial Club and have at the center an urban development strategy based on revitalizing the downtown core and prioritizing the financial, real estate and tourist sectors of the economy while at the same time demolishing public housing and schools in order to gentrify historically African American and Latino working class neighborhoods. These transformations are deeply related to the larger structural crisis of capitalism. The background to this is the crisis of profitability that comes to a head in the early 1970s, and the ushering in [of] a period of capitalist regulation known as neoliberalism, marked by savage attacks on unions, workers and working-class living standards. Reconstructing the built environment of the city has been absolutely central to all of these changes. This is one attempt to deal with the structural crisis of capitalism at this critical juncture. And destroying unions, and teachers' unions in particular, have been key to that attempt.[13]

This is all the more reason for educators and others to address important social issues and to defend public education as a democratic public sphere. And it is all the more reason to defend the Chicago Public Teachers Union in their struggle with Emanuel because this battle is not a local issue. On the contrary, it is a national issue that will set the stage for the future of American public education, which appears to be on its deathbed.

The struggle in Chicago must be understood as part of a larger set of market-driven policies in which everything is now privatized, transformed into "spectacular spaces of consumption," and exposed to the vicissitudes of the national security state.[14] One consequence is the emergence of what the late Tony Judt called an "eviscerated society"—"one that is stripped of the thick mesh of mutual obligations and social responsibilities" characteristic of a viable democracy.[15] This grim reality represents a failure in civic imagination, political will, and democratic power. [16] It is also part of a politics that strips the social of any democratic ideals. This is the very same politics that drives Mayor Emanuel's policies in Chicago around education and a host of other issues. In Emanuel's ideological script, the common good is viewed as either a source of profit or a pathological disturbance. According to Emanuel and his ilk, the archenemies of freedom are the welfare state, unions, and public service workers such as public school teachers. As was evident in the aftermath of the Boston Marathon bombings, law and order is the new language for mobilizing shared fears rather than shared responsibilities, just as war becomes the all-embracing organizing principle for developing a market-driven society and economy.[17]

Neoliberal policies have a long genealogy and have intensified since the late 1970s with a vengeance. As disparities in income, wealth, and power intensify, the unchecked political and cultural influence of the ultra-rich in shaping educational policies becomes more visible and dangerous. As Diane Ravitch points out in her comment on the Gates Foundation and the politics of philanthropy:

> The Gates Foundation, for example, underwrites almost every organization in its quest to control American education. It supports right-wing groups like Jeb Bush's Foundation for Educational Excellence and Ben Austin's Parent Revolution. In the recent past, it gave money to the reactionary ALEC. It pays young teachers to oppose unions and to testify against the rights of tenured teachers. It also pays unions to support its ideas about evaluations, despite their flaws. It spends hundreds of millions of dollars to support "independent" think tanks, which are somewhat less independent when they become dependent on Gates money.[18]

Mayor Emanuel is no stranger to the neoliberal agenda pushed by Arne Duncan, President Obama's secretary of education, or the Gates Foundation and other right-wing corporate groups. Mayor Emanuel supports a notion of educational reform in which pedagogy is often treated simply as a set of strategies and skills to use in order to teach pre-specified subject matter; mathematical measurements are considered the only valid way to account for how, what, and why students learn; and the only questions worth asking about educational policy and pedagogy are determined by commercial forces. Consequently, pedagogy becomes synonymous with teaching as a technique or the practice of a narrow, craft-like skill. Even worse, pedagogy becomes a sterile method for developing skills aimed at raising test scores. Parents, teachers, and other educators must reject this definition of teaching and educational reform along with its endless slavish imitations, even when they claim to be part of an "educational reform" project. In opposition to the instrumental reduction of pedagogy to a method—which has no language for relating the self to public life, social responsibility, or the demands of citizenship—progressive educators need to argue for modes of critical pedagogy that illuminate the relationships among knowledge, authority, and power.[19] For instance, any viable reform movement must raise questions regarding who has control over the conditions for the production of knowledge. Is the production of knowledge and curricula in the hands of teachers and the community or corporate interests?

Central to any democratically informed approach to pedagogy is the recognition that pedagogy is always a deliberate attempt on the part of educators to influence how and what bodies of knowledge and subjectivities are produced within particular sets of social relations. Of crucial importance, then, is the question of authority and how it is legitimated, used, and exercised. When teachers are stripped of authority, pedagogy becomes lifeless, methodical, and militarized, reduced to low-level skills and modes of standardization that debase creativity and cripple the imaginative capacities of both teachers and students. Part of what the Chicago teachers have drawn attention to in their protests against school closings are the ways in which authority, knowledge, power, desire, and experience are produced under specific, basic conditions of learning; in doing so, they have shed light on educational reform movements in which teaching is stripped of its sense of accountability to parents, place, and the complex dynamics of history and communities. Under such circumstances, the Chicago teachers are refusing educational policies in which matters of governance, policy, ideology, and pedagogy are removed from democratic values, norms, and power and subordinated to the neoliberal agenda of testing, accountability, choice, and privatization.

Mayor Emanuel's neoliberal philosophy has no educational understanding of what actually happens in classrooms and other educational settings because it is incapable of raising questions regarding the relationship between learning and social change, what knowledge is of most worth, what it means to know something, and in what direction one should desire. Nor does his philosophy acknowledge that pedagogy is simultaneously about the practices teachers and students might engage in together, along with the knowledge, values, and social relations such practices legitimate. What scares Emanuel and other neoliberal reformers is that pedagogy is a moral and political practice that is always implicated in power relations because it offers particular versions and visions of civic life, community, the future, and how we construct representations of ourselves, others, and our physical and social environment.

At the heart of the Chicago demonstrations against Emanuel's policies is a series of broader questions that situates the right-wing reform movement within the context of market-driven politics. For instance, what kind of society allows economic injustice and massive inequality to run wild and result in drastic cuts to education and public services? Why are more police being put in schools and more prisons being built in the United States? What does it mean when students face not just tuition hikes but a lifetime of financial debt, while their government spends trillions on weapons of death and endless war? What kind of education does it take both in and outside of schools to recognize the various economic, political, cultural, and social forces that point to the dissolution of democracy and the emergence of a new kind of authoritarian state?

In an age of irresponsible privatization and perpetual war, it has become more and more difficult to acknowledge that educators and other cultural workers shoulder an enormous responsibility in opposing the current threat to the society and bringing democratic political culture back to life. Lacking a self-consciously democratic focus or political project, teachers are often reduced to being either technicians or functionaries engaged in formalistic rituals, unconcerned with the disturbing and urgent problems that confront the larger society or the broader consequences of one's pedagogical practices and research undertakings. In opposition to this model, with its claims to and conceit of political neutrality, it is crucial that teachers in Chicago and cities across the United States combine the mutually interdependent roles of critical educator and active citizen. This requires finding ways to connect the practice of classroom teaching with the structural operations of power that currently shape society and to provide the conditions for students to view themselves as critical agents capable of making those who exercise authority and power answerable for their actions.

The role of a critical education is not to train students solely for jobs, but to educate them to question critically the institutions, policies, and values that shape their lives, relationships to others, and myriad connections to the larger world. A critical education in the broadest sense must take up the challenge of teaching students how to be self-reflective, how to thoughtfully and compassionately mediate their relationships to others, and how to reflect critically about the world they inhabit. Simply put, students need an education that prepares them to be creative and critical participants in community and democracy. Equally important is the task facing teacher unions all over America to forge alliances with a range of social movements so that struggles for education are connected to struggles for social provisions, new understandings of politics, and the development of mass movements that can effectively rupture the savage influence of neoliberalism. Under the regime of neoliberalism, education is narrowly defined as preparing young people to work in the global economy. This is a reductionist notion of education embraced by the titans of capital and collapses education into training. It is an education suited for creating replaceable cogs in a disposable machine.

Education is never innocent, and if it is to be understood and problematized as a form of academic labor, then educators must resist calls to depoliticize pedagogy through appeals to scientific objectivity or ideological neutrality masking neoliberal dogmatism. This dogmatism in educational spheres now takes the form of blatant attacks on unions, the dissolution of public schools that largely serve low-income communities of color, the imposition of disciplinary apparatuses that criminalize the behavior of children, and the development of curricula that deaden the mind and soul through a narrow pedagogy of test taking. What is happening in Chicago and other cities in the United States is the production of a pedagogy of repression. This points to the need for educators to rethink the purpose and meaning of education, the crucial importance of pedagogy in a democracy, and the collective struggles that will have to be waged in order for teachers to manage the conditions of their own labor.

Education must be reclaimed as central to any viable notions of citizenship, civic responsibility, and democracy. What Rahm Emmanuel and his ilk fear is the potential of public education to enable students to think critically, hold power accountable, and imagine education as a form of educated hope. Education and pedagogy cannot be reduced to the dictates of an audit culture with its rendering of critical thought nil and void, and its elevation of mindless test taking as the ultimate pedagogical practice and the final arbiter of what constitutes quality teaching and learning. What is lost in this practice is a pedagogy rooted in what it means to be educated—one that provides the conditions for students come to grips with their own power, master the best histories and legacies of education available, learn to think critically, and be willing to hold authority accountable. This is a pedagogy that understands that changing attitudes is not enough and that, most importantly, students should be inspired to exercise their social responsibility as engaged citizens willing to struggle for social, economic, and political justice. Unfortunately, this is the last approach to education that the current mayor of Chicago and other champions of neoliberalism want to see materialize in public schools across the nation.

What Chicago public school teachers fought for in their three days of demonstrations in 2013 was the right to define teaching as a performative practice that encourages young people to be literate and knowledgeable, but also to move beyond simple matters of critique and understanding in order to embrace the mutually informing modalities of power and knowledge. The teachers themselves engaged education as an act of intervention in the world. At the center of the brave struggles waged by the Chicago public school teachers was the essential recognition that any viable approach to pedagogy must acknowledge the crucial nature of the working conditions necessary for teacher autonomy, cooperation, decent classrooms, child safety, and the capacity for teachers and students to enter relations of power in productive ways—ways that point to self-development, self-determination, and social agency.

In the aftermath of the Chicago protests, what educators, parents, and their allies must continue to address is that without power over the conditions of their labor, teachers become pawns in a neoliberal politics in which they are deskilled, reduced to security guards, and work to train instead of educate students. High-stakes testing and its corresponding by-products—degrading forms of competition, rampant cheating among administrators, neglect of special needs students, and the stripping of the civic imagination—emerge from an instrumental rationality and a reification of method that are nothing if not a kind of methodological madness. This is a pedagogy that kills the imagination, moral witnessing, and the sheer pleasure of learning. Soaring heights of creative possibility are replaced by the drudgery of memorization, rote learning, and harsh disciplinary practices. Also in Chicago in 2013, hundreds of students took to the streets protesting standardized testing and how it has been used as a justification to close schools, reward a small subset of teachers, and punish students. Their message: "We are over-tested, under-resourced, and fed up!"[20] Standardized testing is also being protested across the United States in a number of states and local school districts. For instance, as reported by *Democracy Now!*, Seattle teachers who protested standardized testing received support nationally from a number of teacher unions, including the National Education Association and the American Federation of Teachers.

In fact, teachers at Garfield High School waged a successful battle to get the school district to stop administering standardized tests, "calling them wasteful and unfairly used to grade their performance."[21] In what many observers saw as a blow against the Obama administration's aggressive adoption of standardized testing, the boycott was supported by many other Seattle schools and received the widespread backing of teachers, students, and parents.[22]

What needs to be understood is that pedagogy is more than a method or its antithesis—a freewheeling conversation between students and teachers. On the contrary, pedagogy is effective when it recognizes that teaching is always directive: that is, teaching is an act of intervention inextricably mediated through particular forms of authority that enable teachers to offer students—for whatever use they wish to make of them—a variety of analytic and creative tools, diverse historical traditions, a wide range of knowledge, and a way to passionately connect learning to their own lives. At issue here is a practice that must provide the conditions for students to learn to think both creatively and critically, and to narrate themselves. Such a practice must also allow teachers to be learners who are attentive to the histories, knowledge, and experiences that students bring to the classroom and any other sphere of learning. In this instance, pedagogy should empower students to learn how to govern, rather than to be governed.

The war being waged in Chicago against the communities' public schools, teachers, and students is the product of corporate-driven ideologies that numb the mind and the spirit, emphasize repressive modes of learning that promote winning at all costs, discourage questioning authority, and devalue efforts to be thoughtful, innovative, and attentive to the power relations that shape everyday life and the larger world. As learning is increasingly commercialized, depoliticized, and reduced to teaching students how to be good consumers, any remaining notions of the social, public values, citizenship, and democracy wither and die.

What role might public school teachers take in light of poisonous assaults waged on public schools by the forces of neoliberalism? In the most immediate sense, they can raise their collective voices against the influence of corporations that are flooding societies with a culture of war, consumerism, and privatization. They can show how this culture of commodified cruelty and violence is only one part of a broader and all-embracing militarization of society that increasingly disconnects schools from public values, the common good, and democracy itself. They can bring all of their intellectual and collective resources together to critique and dismantle the imposition of high-stakes testing and other commercially driven modes of accountability on schools. They can mobilize young people and others to defend education as a public good by advocating for policies that invest in schools rather than in the military-industrial complex and its massive and expensive weapons of death (like the faulty F35 jets that cost the U.S. government $137 million each). They can educate young people and the broader public to fight against modeling schools after prisons, against installing police and enhanced surveillance techniques, and against implementing zero-tolerance policies that largely punish poor minority children.

Instead of investing in schools, children, health care, jobs for young people, and much-needed infrastructures, neoliberal societies celebrate militarism, hyper-masculinity, extreme competition, and a survival-of-the-fittest ethic while exhibiting disdain for any form of shared bonds, dependency, and compassion for others. Advocates of neoliberalism have cut back social provisions and health care benefits, destroyed pension plans, and allowed inequality to run wild, and have done so in order to safeguard and expand the assets of the rich and powerful. As social bonds and the institutions that support them disappear, so do the formative cultures that make civic education, critical literacy, and cultures of questioning possible.

Too many school systems operate within disciplinary apparatuses that turn public education into an extension of either the prison-industrial complex or the culture of the shopping mall. When not being arrested for trivial rule violations, students are forced to look at walls, buses, and bathrooms that have become giant advertisements for consumer products, many of which are detrimental to the health of students and indeed might be contributing to the obesity crisis in America. Increasingly, even school curricula are organized to reflect the sound of the cash register, hawking products for students to buy and promoting the interests of corporations that celebrate fossil fuels as an energy source, sugar-filled drinks, and a Disney-like view of the world. And, of course, this commodification of public education is migrating to higher education with the speed of light. University student centers are being modeled after department stores, complete with an endless array of vendors trying to sell credit cards to a generation already deep in debt. And on the academic side of things, university faculty are increasingly valued more for their ability to secure grants than for their scholarship.

What is encouraging about the growing opposition of the Chicago teachers to the poisonous policies, mind-numbing pedagogy, and shameless racism of Mayor Rahm Emanuel is their willingness—under the inspiring educational leadership of Karen Lewis, the head of the Chicago Teachers Union—to develop a discourse of both critique and possibility. This has meant developing discourses and practices that connect reading the word with reading the world, and doing so in ways that enhance the capacities of young people as critical agents and engaged citizens. In taking up this project, Lewis and others have worked to create the conditions that give students the opportunities to become critical and engaged citizens who have the knowledge and courage to struggle in order to make desolation and cynicism unconvincing and hope practical. Hope in this instance is educational, removed from the fantasy of an idealism that is unaware of the constraints facing the dream of a democratic society. Educated hope is not a call to overlook the difficult conditions that shape both schools and the larger social order. On the contrary, it is the precondition for providing those languages, values, civic empowerments, and collective struggles that point the way to a more democratic and just world.

Democracy should be foundational to thinking about education—an education that thrives on connecting equity to excellence, learning to ethics, and agency to the imperatives of social responsibility and the public good.[23] Educated hope provides the basis for dignifying the entire community: teachers, students, families, and administrators; it offers up critical knowledge linked to democratic social change; it affirms shared responsibilities and encourages teachers and students to recognize justice, equality, and social responsibility as fundamental dimensions of learning. Such hope offers the possibility of thinking beyond the given. As difficult as this task may seem to educators, if not to a larger public, it is a struggle worth waging.

Right-wing governors, corporate-affiliated politicians, and shameless hedge fund managers and billionaires are exerting every effort in order to further commercialize public education and destroy the dignity of teachers, students, and critical learning. As democracy begins to fail and political life becomes further impoverished through the undermining of vital public spheres such as public and higher education, America loses the civic values, public scholarship, and traditions of social engagement that take seriously the demands of justice and allow for a more imaginative grasp of a future. Yet Chicago teachers refused to believe that the antidemocratic market-driven forces attacking American public schools are irreversible or part of a new common sense that is beyond critical inquiry and dissent. The three days of protest and demonstrations hold a wider meaning for all Americans. Not only do they prove that the future is still open, they indicate that the time has come for acts of moral and political courage that defend public education as crucial to invigorating and fortifying a new era of civic imagination, a renewed sense of social agency, and an impassioned collective political will. Public school teachers are one of the few remaining constituencies that can still imagine the promise of democracy and are willing to fight for it. The struggle waged by Chicago public school teachers is part of a larger battle over the future of education—and democracy itself.

SEVEN

BEYOND THE DISIMAGINATION MACHINE

We've entered a world in which politics has no shape, people don't feel they fully understand the rules of the political system they operate in, hence the sense that what needs to change is to have less of it. That's frightening, because all the precedent that I can think of then points against faith in democracy, rather than the belief in more democracy.[1]

—Tony Judt

We live in a time of deep foreboding, one that haunts any discourse about justice, democracy, and the future. Not only have the points of reference that provided a sense of certainty and collective hope in the past largely evaporated, but the only referents available are increasingly supplied by megacorporations, a corrupt financial services industry, and an increasingly plutocratic political system. The commanding economic and cultural institutions of the United States have taken on what David Theo Goldberg calls a "militarizing social logic."[2] Market discipline now regulates all aspects of social life, and the regressive economic rationality that drives it sacrifices the public good, public values, and social responsibility to a tawdry consumerist dream while simultaneously creating a throwaway society of goods, resources, people, and whole communities.[3] This militarizing logic is also creeping into public schools and colleges, with the former increasingly resembling the culture of prisons and the latter opening their classrooms to the national intelligence agencies.[4] In one glaring instance of universities endorsing the basic institutions of the punishing state, Florida Atlantic University in Boca Raton concluded a deal, later rescinded, to rename to rename its football stadium after the GEO Group, a private prison corporation "whose record is marred by human rights abuses, by lawsuits, by unnecessary deaths of people in their custody and a whole series of incidents."[5] Armed guards are now joined by armed knowledge and militarized naming rights. Corruption, commodification, and repressive state apparatuses have become the central features of a predatory society in which it is presumed irrationally "that markets should dominate and determine all choices and outcomes to the occlusion of any other considerations."[6]

The political, economic, and social consequences have done more than deface any viable vision of a good society. They have undermined the public's capacity to think and act in its own interest. This has entailed the destruction of social protections and a massive shift toward a punitive state that criminalizes the behavior of those bearing the hardships imposed by a survival-of-the-fittest society that takes delight in the suffering of others. How else to account for a criminal justice system stacked overwhelmingly against people of color and a prison system in which "prisoners can be held in solitary confinement for years in small, windowless cells in which they are kept for twenty-three hours of every day"?[7] Or a police state that puts handcuffs on a five-year-old and puts him in jail because he violated a school dress code by wearing sneakers that were the wrong color?[8]

Why does the American public put up with an economic system in which, by 2009, "the top 1 percent of households owned 35.6 percent of net wealth (net worth) and a whopping 42.4 percent of net financial assets," while many young people today represent the "new face of a national homeless population"?[9] America is awash in a culture of civic illiteracy, cruelty, and corruption. For example, major banks such as Barclays and HSBC swindle billions from clients and increase their profit margins by laundering money for terrorist organizations, but no one goes to prison, no one even gets arrested and tried. Even officials within the state apparatus itself, like the inspector general of the Justice Department, Michael E. Horowitz, openly report that the Justice Department had little or no interest in prosecuting the Wall Street criminals at the heart of the mortgage-fraud scandals that plunged the nation into recession and caused economic mass destruction for millions of Americans.[10] At the same time, we have the return of debtor prisons for the poor who cannot pay something as trivial as a parking fine. President Obama arbitrarily decides that he can override due process and kill American citizens through drone strikes and the American public barely blinks. Civic life collapses into a war zone, yet the dominant media are upset only because they were not invited to witness the golf match between Obama and Tiger Woods.

The Violence of Neoliberalism

Virtual culture and real life now feed each other through the relentless marketing of violence as entertainment. The aestheticized carnage in movies such as *Savages*, *A Good Day to Die Hard*, *Django Unchained*, *Only God Forgives*, and *300: Rise of an Empire* increasingly suggests that righteous violence is the only modality left to mediate a society "organized around the brute necessity of survival."[11] The raw, hyped spectacle of bloodshed and gore in popular programs such as *The Walking Dead* portrays civic life as reduced to a zone of abandonment populated by bloodthirsty zombies. Serial killers such as those depicted in the television series *Dexter* and *The Following* are portrayed as far more interesting and complex than their victims. The NBC series *Chicago PD* reinforces the mainstream law-and-order assumption that violence should be accorded the highest priority in mediating relations and solving problems. As Aaron Cantu points out, *Chicago PD* "features a team of intelligence officers who, like some of their real-life counterparts, torture suspects, circumvent civil liberties protections and keep tight-lipped about each other's off-duty violence against innocent people."[12] These spectacles of violence have to be situated within a broader historical context of increasing police violence in the United States in order to understand how the media both resonates with and legitimates such practices. Police violence in an increasing militarized society needs to be condemned, not glamorized, especially when such violence encourages aggressive policing and mimics tactics used in war zones. As Bethania Palma Markus points out, when "police become indistinguishable from troops fighting overseas wars," urban spaces are treated as combat zones, and "residents in American neighborhoods end up being potential 'insurgents.'" [13] All of these shows offer their audiences a spectacle of violence that is amped up in voyeuristic fashion so as to invite them into a pornographic fantasy. What is disturbing is that the entertainment products being marketed bear an uncanny ethical blindness, if not legitimation, for the conditions that spawn the real-life violence being played out in cities across the nation. As violence erupts in American schools, malls, movie theaters, and streets, the American public yawns as popular culture shamelessly markets, packages, and sells such violence, boldly suggesting that its real value lies in harnessing it as a potential cash crop. As the *New York Times* reports, "the top-rated show on cable TV is rife with shootings, stabbings, machete attacks and more shootings. The top drama at the box office fills theaters with the noise of automatic weapons fire. The top-selling video game in the country gives players the choice to kill or merely wound their quarry."[14] Children's cartoons, loaded with weapons, battles, and war, open the way to ultra-violent teen and adult entertainment products.

Murder has become something of a national ritual in America and barely registers in a collective psyche in which the incitement to violence has become the major source of entertainment. As the line between real and fictional violence collapses, a culture is created in which violence becomes acceptable, valued, marketed, and even eroticized. Young people are particularly vulnerable to this, and its effects can be seen in the acceptance of a gun culture in which 561 children age twelve and under were killed by firearms between 2006 and 2010.[15] Violence is now not only a major source of entertainment and vicarious pleasure, but also a most valued approach to mediating conflicts, addressing problems, and defining both a hyped notion of power and U.S. national identity. Bombing Syria, for example, was prioritized before engaging it diplomatically was seriously considered as worthy of a thoughtful and important debate.

Right-wing financiers' lobbyists and media pundits are paid to argue for more guns in order to feed the bottom line even as the senseless carnage continues tragically in places like Newtown, Connecticut, and Tustin, California, as well as other American cities. Liberal politicians such as Democratic senator Barbara Boxer (California) legitimate the youth-control complex by proposing legislation in which $50 million in federal grants would be used to install more metal detectors, security guards, and surveillance cameras in public schools. In the meantime, the mainstream media treat the insane rambling of National Rifle Association's Executive Vice President Wayne LaPierre as a legitimate point of view among many voices. This is the same Wayne LaPierre who, after the killing of twenty young children and six adults at Sandy Hook Elementary School, claimed the only way to stop more tragedies was to flood the market with more guns and provide schools with more armed guards. The American public was largely silent on the issue, in spite of the fact that an increase of police in schools does nothing to prevent such massacres—although it does appear to multiply the number of children, particularly poor black youth, who are pulled out of class, booked, and arrested for trivial behavioral infractions.

America's obsession with weapons and violence is further reinforced by a market society that is Darwinian in its pursuit of profit and personal gain at almost any cost. Within this scenario, a social and economic order has emerged that embodies and amplifies the scenarios of films such as the classic *Mad Max* and *American Psycho*, along with the more recent *The Wolf of Wall Street*. Violence runs through the very capillaries of American culture and reaches back to the founding of the nation itself. As Etienne Balibar points out, what is "perhaps . . . unprecedented is basically the *new visibility of extreme violence*, particularly in the sense that modern techniques of media coverage and broadcasting and the transformation of images . . . transform extreme violence into a *show*, and display this show simultaneously before a world audience."[16]

Material deprivation, galloping inequality, the weakening of public supports, the elimination of viable jobs, the mindless embrace of rabid competition and consumption, and the willful destruction of the environment speak to a society in which militarized violence finds its counterpart, if not legitimating credo, in a set of atomizing and selfish values that disdain shared social bonds and any notion of the public good. As John Le Carré once stated, "America has entered into one of its periods of historical madness."[17] While Le Carré wrote this acerbic attack on American politics in 2003, I think it is fair to say that things have gotten worse and that the United States is further plunging into madness because of a deadening form of historical and social amnesia that has taken over the country, resulting in a massive flight from memory and social responsibility. The politics of disimagination includes, in this instance, what Mumia Abu-Jamal has labeled "mentacide," an erasure of historical memory "inflicted on Black youth by the system's systematic campaign to eradicate and deny them their people's revolutionary history."[18] As Abu-Jamal makes clear, the the varieties of organized forgetting that plague the United States today have particularly deadly consequences for communities of color.

America's Plunge into Militarized Madness

How does one account for the lack of public outcry over millions of Americans losing their homes to corrupt bankers and millions more becoming unemployed because of the lack of an adequate jobs program in the United States, while at the same time stories abound of colossal greed and corruption on Wall Street?[19] For example, in 2009 alone, hedge fund manager David Tepper made approximately $4 billion.[20] As Michael Yates points out, "this income, spent at a rate of $10,000 a day and exclusive of any interest, would last him and his heirs 1,096 years! If we were to suppose that Mr. Tepper worked 2,000 hours in 2009 (fifty weeks at forty hours per week), he took in $2,000,000 per hour and $30,000 a minute."[21] Hedge fund manager Steven Cohen of SAC Capital Advisors took home $1.4 billion in 2012, while Ray Balio, Bridgewater Associates founder, made $1.7 billion.[22]

Paul Buchheit reports that the Charles and David Koch, both "members of the .00001% . . . a group of about twenty individuals . . . have a total net worth of over a half-trillion dollars, about $26 billion each."[23] This degree of concentrated wealth is a direct assault on the social conscience and any viable vestige of democracy, especially when the poorest 47 percent of Americans have no wealth.[24] It gets worse. In 2012, the Koch brothers "made enough money in one second to feed one homeless woman for an entire year."[25] Such colossal individual wealth and unchecked greed are rarely mentioned in the mainstream media, let alone juxtaposed with the deep suffering and misery now experienced by millions of families, workers, children, jobless public servants, and young people. The general neglect of people's distress is especially true in the case of a generation of youth who have become the new precariat[26]—a zero generation relegated to zones of social and economic abandonment, and looking ahead to a future marked by zero jobs, zero hope, and what Zygmunt Bauman has defined as a societal condition that is indefinite and "liquid," but also more punitive and, in the end, death dealing.[27]

Narcissism and sociopathic greed have morphed into more than psychological categories that point to an affliction of the marginal few. Such diseased behaviors are now symptomatic of a plutocratic society in which extremes of violence, militarization, cruelty, and inequality are hardly noticed and have become normalized. Unchecked avarice and egotism are not new. What is new is the unprecedented social submission to the ethos of greed that has emerged since the 1980s.[28] What is also new is that military force and militaristic values have become a source of pride rather than alarm in American society. Not only has the war on terror resulted in the wanton violation of civil liberties, but it has further enabled the military to assume a central role in American society influencing everything from markets, education, and popular culture to high fashion. President Dwight D. Eisenhower left office in 1961 warning Americans about the rise of the military-industrial-complex, with its pernicious alignment of the defense industry, the military, and political power.[29] What he underestimated was the transition from a militarized economy to a militarized society in which the culture itself would be shaped by military power, values, and interests. What has become clear in contemporary America is that the organization of civil society for the production of violence is about more than producing militarized technologies and weapons; it is also about producing militarized subjects and a permanent war economy. As Aaron B. O'Connell points outs:

> Our culture has militarized considerably since Eisenhower's era, and civilians, not the armed services, have been the principal cause. From lawmakers' constant use of "support our troops" to justify defense spending, to TV programs and video games like "NCIS," "Homeland" and "Call of Duty," to NBC's shameful and unreal reality show "Stars Earn Stripes," Americans are subjected to a daily diet of stories that valorize the military while

the storytellers pursue their own opportunistic political and commercial agendas.[30]

The imaginary of war and violence now informs every
aspect of American society, and extends from the celebration of a wartime culture in mainstream media to the use
of universities to indoctrinate students in the logic of the
national security state. Military deployments now protect
"fair trade" arrangements, provide job programs, and drain
revenue from public coffers. For instance, the aerospace giant and defense contractor Lockheed Martin stands to gain
billions of dollars in profit as Washington prepares to buy
2,443 of its F-35 fighter planes at a cost of $207.6 million
each. The overall project cost for the planes has been called
a "one trillion dollar boondoggle" and is expected to total
more "than Australia's entire GDP ($924 billion)."[31] Yet the
American government displays no qualms about cutting
food programs for the poor, early childhood programs for
low-income students, and food stamps for those who exist
below the poverty line. Nor is there a public outcry when
the Chicago Public Schools system "spends $51.4 million on
security guards, but only $3.5 million for college and career
coaches."[32] Such misplaced priorities represent more than a
military-industrial complex that is out of control. They also
suggest the plunge of American society into the dark abyss
of state governance that is increasingly punitive, organized
around the production of violence, and unethical in its policies, priorities, and values.

John Hinkson argues that such institutionalized violence is far from being limited to a short-lived and aberrant historical moment. In fact, he rightfully asserts that "we have a new world economy, one that crucially lacks all substantial points of reference and is by implication nihilistic. The point is that this is not a temporary situation because of the imperatives, say, of war: it is a structural break with the past."[33] As John Atcheson has similarly pointed out using a different benchmark for comparison, we are "witnessing an epochal shift in our socio-political world. We are de-evolving, hurtling headlong into a past that was defined by serfs and lords; by necromancy and superstition; by policies based on fiat, not facts."[34] Evidence of such a shift—perhaps reminiscent of the medieval past yet manifest today on an unprecedented scale—can be seen in the massive upward transfer of wealth and income that has not only resulted in the concentration of power in relatively few hands, but also promoted unprecedented degrees of human suffering and hardship along with what I call a politics of disimagination.

We are plunging into a dark world of anti-intellectualism, civic illiteracy, and a formative culture conditioned to comply with the violations of privacy and power imposed by state surveillance and authoritarianism. The embrace of ignorance is at the center of political life today, and reactionary forms of mass media and public pedagogy have become powerful forces of indoctrination. Civic illiteracy is the modus operandi for depoliticizing the population and disarming it of the ability to recognize, articulate, and advance its own interests. In an educated democracy, much of the debate that occupies political life today—from creationism and climate change denial to "birther" arguments—would be speedily dismissed as magical thinking, superstition, and an obvious form of witlessness.

Mark Slouka is right in arguing that "ignorance gives us a sense of community; it confers citizenship; our representatives either share it or bow down to it or risk our wrath. . . . Communicate intelligently in America and you're immediately suspect."[35] The machinery of disimagination and its production of ever-deepening political illiteracy dominate American society because they generate, to a large degree, uninformed citizens, hapless clients, and self-centered publics incapable of holding corporate and political power accountable. In an educated democracy, society would not revolve around the corporation but around the school, the library, the plaza, the airwaves, the parks and other noncommercial institutions that defend and advance the health, intelligence, environment, and egalitarian processes necessary for society to thrive.

Toward a Radical Imagination

Against the politics of disimagination, progressives, workers, educators, young people and others need to develop a new language of radical reform and create new public spheres that provide the pedagogical conditions for critical thought, dialogue, and thoughtful deliberation. At stake here is a notion of pedagogy that both informs the mind and creates the conditions for modes of agency that are critical, informed, engaged, and socially responsible. The radical imagination can be nurtured around the merging of critique and hope, the capacity to connect private troubles with broader social considerations, and the production of alternative formative cultures that provide the preconditions for political engagement and for mobilizing democratic movements toward social change—movements willing to think beyond isolated struggles and the limits of a today's operative form of predatory capitalism. Frances Fox Piven, Rick Wolfe, Stanley Aronowitz and others point to such a project in their manifesto on the radical imagination. They write:

> This Manifesto looks forward to the creation of a new political Left formation that can overcome fragmentation, and provide a solid basis for many-sided interventions in the current economic, political and social crises that afflict people in all walks of life. The Left must once again offer to young people, people of color, women, workers, activists, intellectuals and newly arrived immigrants places to learn how the capitalist system works in all of its forms of exploitation whether personal, political, or economic. We need to reconstruct a platform to oppose Capital. It must ask in this moment of U.S. global hegemony what are the alternatives to its cruel power over our lives, and those of large portions of the world's peoples. And the Left formation is needed to offer proposals on how to rebuild a militant, democratic labor movement, strengthen and transform the social movements; and, more generally, provide the opportunity to

obtain a broad education that is denied to them by official institutions. We need a political formation dedicated to the proposition that radical theory and practice are inextricably linked, that knowledge without action is impotent, but action without knowledge is blind.[36]

Matters of justice, equality, and political participation are foundational to any functioning democracy. Yet, as the manifesto suggests, it is equally important to recognize that radical change will have to be rooted in a vibrant formative culture in which democracy is understood not just as a political and economic structure, but also as an educational force producing new modes of thinking about justice, equality, and freedom. While the institutions and practices of a civil society and an aspiring democracy are essential in this project, what must also be present are the principles and modes of civic education and critical engagement that support the very foundations of democratic culture and enable it to flourish. Central to such a project will be the development of a new radical imagination both through the pedagogies and projects of public intellectuals in the academy and through work that can be done in other educational sites such as electronic media. Utilizing the Internet, social media, and other elements of digital and screen culture, educators, cultural workers, young people, and others can address larger audiences and begin the task of challenging diverse forms of oppression, exploitation, and exclusion as part of a broader effort to create a radical democracy.

As this suggests, the American public must confront the urgent need to invent modes of pedagogy that release the imagination, connect learning to social change, and create social relations in which people assume responsibility for each other. Such a pedagogy is not about methods or prepping students to learn how to take tests. Nor is such an education about imposing harsh disciplinary behaviors in the service of the surveillance state. On the contrary, it is about a moral and political practice capable of energizing students and others to become more knowledgeable, while creating the conditions for generating a new vision of the future in which people can recognize themselves—a vision that resonates with the desires, dreams, and hopes of all those who are willing to fight for and participate in a community-driven democracy.

Americans need to develop a new understanding of civic literacy, education, and engagement, one capable of developing a new conversation and a new political project about democracy, inequality, and the redistribution of wealth and power and how such a discourse can offer the conditions for democratically inspired visions, modes of governance, and profit making. Americans need to restore modes of civic literacy, critical education, and democratic social movements as forms of national wealth where dissent can be produced, public values asserted, dialogue made meaningful, and critical reflection embraced as a noble ideal.

Elements of such a utopian imaginary rooted in critical thought is on full display in Martin Luther King Jr.'s "Letter from Birmingham City Jail," in which King states under the weight and harshness of incarceration that an "injustice anywhere is a threat to justice everywhere" and asks: will we "be extremists for the preservation of injustice—or will we be extremists for the cause of justice?" [37] According to King, "we must use time creatively, and forever realize that the time is always ripe to do right. Now is the time to make real the promise of democracy." [38] The utopian imaginary can also be found in James Baldwin's "Open Letter to My Sister, Angela Davis," in which he points out that "we live in an age in which silence is not only criminal but suicidal." [39] We hear it in the words of former Harvard University president James B. Conant who makes an impassioned case for "the need for the American radical—the missing political link between the past and future of this great democratic land." [40] We hear it in the voices of young people all across the United States—the new American radicals—who are fighting for a society in which justice matters, social protections are guaranteed, equality is ensured, and education becomes a right and not an entitlement. The radical imagination waits to be unleashed through social networks and movements where collective desires for civic sovereignty and economic justice once again become the driving force behind agency, hope, and the struggle for greater democracy and community.

We need new vocabularies for resistance and solidarity against the violence of the militarized state and the market, ones that embrace freedom as more than the need to shop or, for that matter, as more than a libertarian concept that is empty of any meaning. Freedom becomes a bankrupt notion when it is removed from the material and symbolic constraints that shape its possibilities as collective experience and a foundational element of democratic agency. What sites are left for fighting against the disimagination machine? We see the promise of such sites in the new media, the alternative press, the uprisings and models of democratic participatory engagement being generated by youthful protesters all over the world, though we rarely look to higher education for interventions and inspiration. It is to a consideration of higher education in these terms that I want to turn now.

At a time when higher education is under siege all over the globe by market mentalities and moralities, there is an urgent necessity on the part of the American public to reclaim the academy in its multiple forms as a site of critique and a public good, one that connects knowledge and power, scholarship and public life, and pedagogy and civic engagement. The current assault on higher education makes clear that it should not be reduced in value to cost-benefit analyses or harnessed to the singular needs of corporations, which often leads to the loss of egalitarian and democratic pressures. Universities should be about more than developing work-related skills; they should be about life and the search for knowledge and meaning. They must also be about producing civic-minded and critically engaged citizens—citizens who can engage in debate, dialogue, and bear witness to a different and critical sense of remembering, agency, ethics, and collective resistance. Universities are one of the few places left where a struggle for the commons and for public life, if not democracy itself, can be made visible through the media of collective voices and social movements.

As the prospects for social progress and welfare continue to be attacked and the punishing state increasingly criminalizes social issues—extending from homelessness and peaceful protest to dress code violations in public schools—academics and other cultural workers should not, under the guise of professionalism, remove themselves from ethical considerations and the power relations that impact them and the world. Nor should they claim a lack of interest at a time when the very concepts of justice, equality, freedom, and democracy are actively traded for the forces of privatization, consumerism, unchecked individualism, and "a political culture of hyper punitiveness."[41]

The university likewise should not collude with the ongoing assaults against social provisions that are waged by policy makers who view marginalized populations as disposable—as waste products of a society that would rather warehouse its citizens, particularly poor minorities, in dilapidated schools and prisons than provide them with decent social protections, health care, jobs, a quality education, and a future that matters. [42] Hence, one goal of those concerned about creating engaged citizens capable of struggling for a radical democracy and against state violence and endless war is to develop new pedagogical practices and modes of civic literacy that connect rigorous scholarship to important social issues, such as the war being waged on youth today, the increasing militarization of all aspects of society, the attack on the welfare state, the growing assault on women's civil and reproductive rights, and the escalating destruction of the environment.

There is a need to reclaim those vibrant ideologies, legacies, and struggles that served and continue to serve as a reminder of how important the liberal arts are, not just as specific fields of study, but also as a broader educational force that enables the development of the formative civic culture necessary for all students to enliven the imagination, think critically, recognize the ethical grammar of suffering, and connect public values to collective struggles that expand and deepen the processes of democracy. Informing such a project would be an attempt to develop a language of critique and possibility, one that recognizes that education is, in part, a moral and political practice whose mission, as the poet Robert Hass points out, "is to refresh the idea of justice going dead in us all the time." [43]

We find ourselves at an important historical moment in which there is a need to reclaim the most robust and democratic versions of the discourses of freedom, justice, collective struggle, and history. Americans occupy a historical conjuncture in which everything that matters politically, ethically, and culturally is being erased—either ignored, turned into a commodity, or simply falsified. Occasionally we are confronted with the unsullied images, historical memory, and legacy of intellectuals who symbolize a rare combination of civic courage, political commitment, and rigorous scholarship. Angela Y. Davis is one of those exemplary activists and engaged intellectuals whose work has not only consistently organized against racial and economic injustice, but who has demonstrated for most of her life what it means to combine politics and commitment, courage and rigorous theoretical work, while combining the power to agitate and organize with the power to educate and enlighten. In addition, she has refused the trap of sectarian single-issue politics and has chosen to participate in broader social movements and collective struggles that engage education as the heart of community building, activism and transformative politics. As a modern-day abolitionist, she is truly an enemy of the disimagination machine because she has always embraced the ability of people to shape their own futures and firmly believes that the struggle over agency is tantamount to the struggle over meaning, subjectivity, and power. In the words of Martin Luther King Jr., she has never been afraid to break the silence and has provided a model of what it means to dismantle the machineries of war, racism, poverty, sexism, and violence that haunt the American landscape. Hence, it is crucial in any talk about disimagination to include insights drawn from her life and work.

The Visionary Courage of Angela Y. Davis

A well-known public intellectual and political activist since the 1960s, Angela Davis has struggled bravely and with great dignity for decades to demonstrate that education is a form of political intervention in the world and that learning is not about processing received knowledge, but actually transforming it as part of a more expansive struggle for individual rights and social justice. She has worked in difficult and shifting circumstances to remind us of the power of education as a central element of inspired self-government. Her scholarship and activism demonstrate the educational force of political and intellectual commitment in its attempts to enlighten the mind and create powerful social movements against a wide range of oppressions. What is particularly crucial about her legacy is that it not only focuses on specific issues, but also addresses society at large, flatly rejecting identitarian politics. Her work advances, as Robin D. G. Kelley points out, a *democratic notion of freedom*, one that moves far beyond the narrow liberal notion of liberty that enshrines the right of the individual to do what he or she wants, unchecked by any impediments, moral or otherwise.[44] Instead Davis combines individual rights with social rights and argues that any viable notion of agency is impossible without providing the economic and social conditions that enable people to exercise their political and individual rights. She argues that freedom is about providing choices for people without the constraints that are imposed by subjugation, deprivation, and the type of inequality evident in the fact that "for every one dollar of assets owned by a single black or Hispanic woman, a member of the Forbes 400 has over forty million dollars."[45]

Freedom in this context is freedom that comes with the struggle against injustice, a struggle that demands the shared conditions that would ensure that all people could live a fully realized life. Collective freedom is one devoid of material bondage and one that supports the institutions necessary for democracy. In this notion of freedom, education is linked to the struggle for a democratic conception of community, one that is inclusive and provides decent health care, housing, food, and education, while abolishing the prison-industrial complex and the ever-expanding surveillance state. Collective freedom provides the basic conditions for people to narrate their own lives, hold power accountable, and embrace a capacious notion of human dignity. Davis's notion of freedom rejects the neoliberal understanding of freedom as the conditions necessary for the rich to get richer without public accountability or interference by the government, and the freedom to pursue one's own private interests, regardless of the social or ecological consequences. This is a notion that depoliticizes freedom in the name of greed, corporate power, unchecked individualism, and pernicious consumerism.

Freedom at its best speaks to both a condition and a practice. As a condition, it acknowledges that no viable mode of self-determination can develop without the social and economic conditions that free people from the material deprivations that cripple matters of choice, power, and agency. As a practice, freedom is the ability not only to understand the world, but to act on that understanding and be able to shape the commanding forces that bear down on one's life. Freedom is always part of an ongoing struggle for new subjects, collective agents, and social movements that embrace the individual but organize collectively. The weight, if not burden, of freedom cannot be understood in the privatized language of megacorporations and the ultra-rich, but in the discourses and struggles of social movements that fight for the egalitarian practices of economic justice, racial equality, and the common good. Angela Davis's legacy as a political activist made her an enemy of the state under the regimes of Nixon, Reagan, and J. Edgar Hoover because she understood that the struggle for freedom was not only a struggle for political and individual rights but also for economic rights. She is much more than an icon; she is a movement builder and freedom fighter who has given most of her life to join with the dispossessed and excluded in the struggle for freedom and emancipatory community.

What is invaluable about Angela Davis's work is that she does not limit her politics to issues removed from broader social considerations, but connects every aspect of her scholarship and public interventions to what the contours of a truly democratic society might look like. For her, democracy is not only a promise and an ideal but also a practice. Angela Davis is a model for what it means to be a public and engaged intellectual dedicated to what she calls "protracted struggles [that refuse] the pitfalls of the particular version of democracy represented by U.S. capitalism."[46] I can think of no one who embodies the commitment to theoretical rigor, social justice, human dignity, and collective resistance more so than Angela Davis. We have a lot to learn from her work: her struggles over the last few decades, her humility and bristling intelligence, and her insistence that pedagogy is the formative basis of not just dissent but collective struggle. Angela Davis represents the *other* America, the America waiting in the shadows to be born again, waiting to once again to tip the scales of justice toward a new ethical horizon, waiting to address and take seriously the promise of a democracy to come, waiting to create the conditions in which the radical imagination challenges and displaces the disimagination machine.

EIGHT

HOPE IN TIME OF PERMANENT WAR

Revolution is not 'showing' life to people, but making them live. A revolutionary organization must always remember that its objective is not getting its adherents to listen to convincing talks by expert leaders, but getting them to speak for themselves, in order to achieve, or at least strive toward, an equal degree of participation.

—Guy Debord

A nation that continues year after year to spend more money on military defense than on programs of social uplift is approaching spiritual death.

—Martin Luther King Jr.

Despite the normalization of authoritarianism, plutocracy, and war, hope and resistance endure. But how? How might it be possible to advance movements and communities of hope and resistance in a country that commercializes violence as entertainment but increasingly considers questioning authority a suspicious act, holds people in indefinite detention at Guantánamo Bay for over a decade, regularly bombs Afghanistan, Pakistan, Somalia, and Yemen, killing civilians on a regular basis, invades the privacy and rights of its own citizens by spying on them and extending the reach of the surveillance state into all aspects of society, and inflicts violence through racial profiling and the machinery of mass incarceration? How does one advance hope while atrocities are being committed on an ongoing basis? Where does hope resist a disimagination machine that deters and erases public memory as it commercializes, monitors, and militarizes every facet of public and private life?

Where is hope when the police are allowed to handcuff a kindergarten student for doodling on her desk or arrest a student for a dress code violation but not the bankers who commit financial crimes that literally rob people of their homes and life savings through predatory loans and foreclosure abuse? What does hope mean in a country in which there is little tolerance for the free speech of people who protest and infinite tolerance for the acts of economic and ecological mass destruction perpetrated by the wealthy elite and those they employ to do their bidding—bankers, hedge fund managers, collection agencies, politicians, lobbyists, and media producers? How can hope make a difference in a country in which money drives politics and getting ahead at any cost replaces notions of community and respect for the public good? Where is the indignation that signals a renewed sense of being on the side of a different and most just future?

What does hope mean when the United States is virtually unmatched around the world for incarcerating thousands of young people of color and destroying millions of families and the social bonds that give them meaning? What does hope teach us at a time when government lies and deception are exposed on a daily basis in the media and yet appear to have little effect on challenging the deeply authoritarian attacks on civil liberties initiated by the president of the United States? What happens to the promise of hope as a foundation for social struggle when all of social life is subordinated to the violence of a deregulated market and the privatization of public resources, including health care, education, and transportation? What resources and visions does hope offer in a society in which profit and possessions are the most important measure of personal achievement?

What is the relevance of hope at a time when most attempts to interrupt the operations of an incipient fascism appear to fuel a growing cynicism rather than promote widespread individual and collective acts of resistance? Where does hope live in a country in which egalitarianism and mutual aid are valued less than self-promotion, hype, and celebrity? How can one imagine hope under a regime of savage neoliberalism in which the mechanisms of domination are not limited to the market but extend into all aspects of social life as part of an ongoing attempt to colonize needs, desires, and subjectivities as mere instruments of the market? Despite all the forces aligned against it, hope is alive and well all over the globe, especially in those places where young people refuse the dictates of authoritarians and the savagery of predatory capitalism and its politics of austerity.

More corrosive than authoritarianism is a loss of faith in the possibilities and promise of collective struggle for an open society, the promise of a community-driven democracy, and a society that is never just enough. In this regard, Robert Reich's comments on an exchange with his mentor are instructive for how to understand the power of militant hope. He writes: "You've been fighting for social justice for over half a century. Are you discouraged?" "Not at all!" he said. "Don't confuse the urgency of attaining a goal with the urgency of fighting for it."[1]

Hope refuses the cynical and politically reactionary idea that power can be simply equated with domination. It also raises serious questions about its own possible demise and the dystopian forces at work in either dismantling or subverting its power to advance democratic agency and social engagement. As a mode of self-reflection, hope raises questions about the growing sense that politics in American life has become corrupt, that progressive social change is a distant memory, and that a discourse of possibility is on the verge of becoming the last refuge of deluded romantics. Those traditional public spheres in which people could exchange ideas, debate, and shape the conditions that structured their everyday lives appear increasingly to have little substance where they still exist, let alone political importance. As Doreen Massey points out, the vocabulary of neoliberalism, with its emphasis on "customer, consumer, choice, markets and self-interest moulds both our conception of ourselves and our understanding of and relationship to the world."[2] One consequence is the erosion of those older social bonds, public values, the social wage, and those institutions vital to a democracy. Moreover, as Stuart Hall argued, "The breakdown of old forms of social solidarity is accompanied by the dramatic growth of inequality and a widening gap between those who run the system or are well paid as its agents, and the working poor, unemployed, under-employed or unwell."[3] Civic engagement seems irrelevant and public values are rendered invisible, if not overtly disparaged, in light of the growing power of multinational corporations to privatize public space and time as it disconnects power from issues of equity, social justice, and civic responsibility. Political exhaustion and impoverished intellectual visions are fed by the widely popular assumption that there are no alternatives to the present state of affairs.

State violence against any display of moral courage and dissent by artists, intellectuals, journalists, and ordinary citizens has become normalized and has sent a chilling effect throughout a society in which all worldly criticism is equated with treason, anti-Americanism, or worse. Whistle-blowers who expose government wrongdoings are labeled as traitors in the dominant media and by the government. As the ACLU has written in its comments on Chelsea Manning, justice and the value of dissent are turned upside down:

> When a soldier who shared information with the press and public is punished far more harshly than others who tortured prisoners and killed civilians, something is seriously wrong with our justice system. A legal system that doesn't distinguish between leaks to the press in the public interest and treason against the nation will not only produce

unjust results, but will deprive the public of critical information that is necessary for democratic accountability.[4]

Americans are now gently coerced to live in an ad-infested bubble of intense privatization, commodification, and civic illiteracy. The public does not merely dissolve into the private, the private is all that is left. Far from simply an economic system, neoliberalism provides a totalizing system of a pay-as-you-go society in which money is speech, politics, and leadership. Those without money are voiceless, openly unrepresented in any political campaign, and forced to pay a terrible price in what Zygmunt Bauman calls the "hard currency of human suffering."[5]

The American public yawns as they are inundated with statistics that should shock, and they are complacent in the face of information that should make them flush with indignation. Politicians accountable to only corporate interests plan for more highly profitable wars, and academics retreat into a vocabulary of social and political irrelevance, while the social movements that attempt to connect these to other big picture issues are monitored, attacked, and fragmented by surveillance and other authoritarian deterrents.

Statistics that should make us outraged reveal the widespread nature of our neighbors' suffering and offer a glimpse of the despair that accompanies an authoritarian society. For example, in the richest country in the world, the "U.S. ranked 27th out of 30 for child poverty," "over 350,000 Americans with advanced degrees applied for food stamps in 2010," millions of young people are crushed under the burden of student loans, increasing numbers of youth are homeless, living on the streets, and over fifty million Americans are uninsured.[6] Inequalities in income, education, nutrition, access to medical attention, and legal assistance have created a country filled with gated communities on the one hand and derelict zones of abandonment and voiceless suffering on the other.[7] The middle class pays higher taxes than many corporations, while the super-rich get even richer. For instance, "each of the Koch brothers saw his investments grow by $6 billion in one year, which is three million dollars per hour based on a 40-hour 'work' week."[8] Equally obscene and symptomatic is the example of Lloyd Blankfein, the chief executive of Goldman Sachs, who made $21 million last year and received a bonus of $5 million in January 2013. At the same time, the least fortunate 47 percent have no wealth, 146 million Americans or 1 in 2 are low income or poor, and a "third of families with young children are now in poverty."[9]

Unlike some theorists who suggest that politics as a site of contestation, critical exchange, and engagement has either come to an end or is in a state of terminal deterrence, especially in light of the well-documented coordinated surveillance and repression of the Occupy movement, I believe that the current state of sub-prime politics points to the urgent challenge of reformulating the crisis of democracy and the radical imagination as part of the fundamental crisis of vision, meaning, education, and political agency. Politics devoid of vision degenerates into either cynicism or appropriates a view of power equated with domination. Lost from such accounts is the recognition that democracy has to be struggled over, even in the face of a most appalling crisis of educational opportunity and political agency.

There is also too little attention paid to the fact that the struggle over politics and democracy is strongly connected to creating and sustaining public spheres where individuals can be engaged as political agents equipped with the skills, capacities, and knowledge they need not only to actually perform as autonomous political agents, but also to believe that such struggles are worth taking up. The formative cultures, institutions, and modes of critical agency necessary for a vibrant democracy do not exist in a culture in which knowledge is fragmented, power concentrated in few hands, and time reduced to a deprivation for large segments of the public—one consequence of which is the endless struggle by many Americans to simply survive at the level of everyday life. The commercial colonization of time, space, and consciousness occurs in parallel with most of the population's need to work more than ever in order to make ends meet. There is no democracy in a country in which for most people time is a deprivation rather than a luxury. Time is crippled when it is trapped within an endless need to fight to merely survive in order to have enough to eat, have access to decent health care, day care, and a social wage. The struggle over time is inextricably linked to a struggle over space, institutions, public spheres, the public good, power, the future, and the nature of political governance itself.

In a country in which the social contract is dissolving,

the social wage is being eviscerated, and social protections are viewed as a pathology, democracy becomes a shadow of itself and choice becomes impotent and an empty slogan because of the constraints imposed on the 99 percent by vast inequalities in wealth, income, power, and opportunity. The growth of cynicism in American society may say less about the reputed apathy of the populace than it might about the bankruptcy of the old political languages and the need for a new language and vision for clarifying intellectual, ethical, and political projects, especially as they work to reframe questions of agency, ethics, and meaning for a substantive democracy. As Zygmunt Bauman has argued, "hope nowadays feels frail, vulnerable, and fissiparous precisely because we can't locate a viable and sufficiently potent agency that can be relied on to make the words flesh."[10] If democratic agents are in short supply so is the formative culture that is necessary to create them—revealing a cultural apparatus that is more than an economic entity or industry. It is also an all-embracing totality of educational sites that produces particular narratives about the world, what it means to be a citizen, and what role education will play in a powerful and unchecked military-industrial-security-surveillance state. Stanley Aronowitz is right in arguing that:

> [The] social character has become entwined with communications technology. . . . This intricate interlock between cultural institutions, political power and everyday life constitutes a new moment of history. It has become the primary machinery

of domination. And a central aspect of domination is the abrogation of concept that we can know the totality, but are condemned to understand the division of the world as a series of specializations. Thus, the well-known fragmentation of social life is both a result of the re-arrangement of social space and the modes by which knowledge is produced, disseminated and ingested. The cultural apparatus is largely responsible for the intellectual darkness that has enveloped us.[11]

We live in a world in which any viable notion of hope has to recognize that social media, or the cultural apparatus as C. W. Mills once acknowledged, has "formed a new mass sensibility, a new condition for the widespread acceptance of the capitalist system" and that our social character has become inextricably merged and shaped by the new social media.[12] Most importantly, the existing cultural apparatuses in all of their diversity are the most powerful educational tools currently shaping not only individual desires, dreams, needs, and fears but the nature of our understanding of politics and social life in general. Yet such cultural apparatuses that range from traditional radio and print to the ever-evolving platforms of the Internet constitute one of the few spheres left in which hope can be nourished through the production and circulation of alternative knowledge, ideas, values, dreams, desires, and modes of subjectivity. The fight over culture may be the most significant that can be waged in the name of hope for a more just and sustainable future.

As power is separated from politics, it becomes more reckless, arrogant, and death-dealing. No longer viewed as accountable, casino capitalism and its minions turn savage in their pursuit of wealth and the means to hoard it. All bets are off and everything is fodder for increasing the wealth of the financial elite and those paid to do their bidding. Ensconced in culture of cruelty, neoliberal power relations have become global, eschewing any sense of responsibility to an ethics of care, justice, and spiritual well-being. Responsibility now floats like a polluted cloud signaling a dystopian future—a symbol of both extreme savagery and corporate irresponsibility. But there is more at work here than a retreat into cynicism or a collective silence in the face of a normalizing disimagination machine. There is a need to craft a new language that requires a more realistic, urgent, and militant sense of emancipatory vision and hope. Hope, in this instance, is the precondition for individual and community social struggle, involving the ongoing practice of critical education in a wide variety of sites and the renewal of civic courage among citizens who wish to address and solve the host of interconnected social, political, and ecological problems imposed by the current system.

Hope is not an individual fantasy or a recourse to a romanticized and unrealistic view of the world. On the contrary, it is a subversive force that enables those who care about humanity, dignity, and ecological sustainability to act in concrete ways to defend and advance them. In opposition to those who seek to turn hope into a new slogan or punish and dismiss efforts to look beyond the horizon of the given, activists, progressives, immigrants, and ordinary people at all levels need to energize a language of resistance and possibility, a language in which hope is viewed as both a project and a condition for turning things around. As a project, Andrew Benjamin insists, hope must be viewed as "a structural condition of the present rather than as the promise of a future, the continual promise of a future that will always have to have been better."[13] Rather than viewed as an individual proclivity, hope must be seen as part of a broader politics that acknowledges those social, economic, spiritual, and cultural conditions in the present that make certain kinds of agency and democratic politics possible.

The late philosopher Ernst Bloch rightly argued that hope must be concrete, a spark that not only reaches out beyond the surrounding emptiness of capitalist relations, anticipating a better world in the future, a world that speaks to us by presenting tasks based on the challenges of the present time. For Bloch, hope becomes concrete when it links the possibility of the "*not yet*" with forms of political agency animated by a determined effort to engage critically with the past and present in order to address pressing social problems and realizable tasks.[14] Bloch believes that hope cannot be removed from the world and is not "something like nonsense or absolute fancy; rather it is *not yet* in the sense of a possibility; that it could be there if we could only do something for it."[15] As a discourse of critique and social transformation, hope in Bloch's view foregrounds the crucial relationship between critical education and political agency, on the one hand, and the concrete struggles needed, on the other, to give substance to the recognition that every present is incomplete. This is a discourse that must be reclaimed, used, and mobilized in the interest of a radical hope willing to struggle collectively, take risks, and make education central to any viable notion of transformative politics.

A discourse of critique and possibility points to a particularly important role for higher education, which is one of the few public spheres left where educators and students can create the conditions for critical thinking, informed dialogue, and a culture of questioning that focuses on both how power undermines decent human communities and also how it can be used collectively to face such problems and to overcome them. As Robert Jensen argues, we need a university "that refuses to serve power and instead focuses its resources on the compelling questions of social justice and ecological sustainability."[16] The university is currently under attack by the ultra-rich and powerful because it is a public sphere where critical thinking, engaged scholarship, and resistance are still possible. Higher education is one of the few remaining places where hope translates into creating the pedagogical conditions in which students can critically interrogate neoliberal assumptions in which the pursuit of personal gain is the organizing principle of a democracy and the claim that a market society and democracy are one and the same. Or for that matter, the injurious assumption that society should be subordinated to market forces.

Neoliberal ideology is poisonous to a healthy democracy not only because it produces unbridled corporate power, exploits cheap labor, creates environmental degradation, constructs a mass incarceration state, and generates crippling levels of poverty and inequality, among other injustices, but also because it conceals its reactionary ideology through an appeal to common sense, thus producing an unquestioned mantra that allegedly "transcends all worldly criticism."[17] As a form of public pedagogy, neoliberalism works through a number of cultural apparatuses extending from film, newspapers, and television to the Internet and ever-evolving social media in order to shape a new popular imagination and manufacture a social consensus that constructs the subjects, values, social relations, and entrepreneurial identities so crucial to a hyper-commercialized society. Neoliberalism as a form of public pedagogy reworks commonsense assumptions of the past, transforming entire worldviews about the meaning of freedom, progress, growth, possessive individualism, the subordination of the public to the private, and the role of the state, among other issues. Under the banner of common sense, competitive individualism replaces any democratic form of solidarity, citizens are now defined as consumers of products, gaining economic advantage is more important than contributing to the common good, and the drive for instant gratification relegates moral responsibility to an outdated principle. One outcome of this dehumanizing value system is the refashioning of the self in market terms that not only produces a neurotic form of atomization, but also a predatory culture of intolerance, cruelty, and abuse. Neoliberalism is not merely an economic system but a cultural apparatus and pedagogy that are instrumental in forming "a new mass sensibility, a new condition for the widespread acceptance of the capitalist system, even the general belief in its eternity."[18] Seeking to hide its ideological and constructed nature, neoliberal ideology attempts through its massive cultural apparatuses to produce an unquestioned common sense that hides its basic assumptions so as to prevent them from being questioned.

Moral witnessing, civic courage, and sustained resistance matter more than ever in American society. We can see the power of collective hope in the increasing resistance by unions, workers, activists and young people to the attack on all things public in Wisconsin, North Carolina, Maine, and other states now controlled by right-wing Republican extremists. In this instance, the longing for a more humane society does not collapse into a retreat from the world but emerges out of critical and practical engagements with present policies, institutional formations, and everyday practices. Hope in this context does not ignore the worse dimensions of human suffering, exploitation, and social relations; on the contrary, it acknowledges the need to sustain the "capacity to see the worst and offer more than that for our consideration."[19] This reclaiming of hope from the consolidation of neoliberalism and the surveillance state that enforces it is a crucial element for the reclamation of not just hope but a fundamental element of politics itself.

Hence, hope is more than a politics, it is also the outcome of those social practices and struggles that tap public memory and community experiences while at the same time linking individual and community responsibilities with a sense of social improvement and change. As a form of social longing, democratic hope opens up horizons of comparison by evoking not just different histories but different public memories and futures; at the same time, it substantiates the importance of ambivalence while problematizing certainty, or, as Paul Ricoeur has suggested, it serves as "a major resource as the weapon against closure."[20] Democratic hope is a subversive force when it pluralizes politics by opening up a space for dissent, making authority accountable, becoming an activating presence in promoting social transformation.

Organized forgetting and the current limits of the social imagination are related, in part, to the failure of intellectuals, academics, artists, cultural workers, educators, and civil society as a whole to imagine and pursue strategies for winning back greater public resources and democratic freedoms. At the same time, a politics and pedagogy of hope is neither a blueprint for the future nor a form of social engineering, but a belief that different futures are possible, holding open matters of contingency, context, and indeterminacy. It is only through critical forms of education that human beings can learn about the limits of the present and the conditions necessary for them to "combine a gritty sense of limits with a lofty vision of possibility."[21] Equally crucial is the belief that hope needs to translate into collective struggles and disciplined social movements which go beyond popular protest and what Aronowitz calls "signs without organization."[22] Such struggles are crucial in order to develop disciplined national organizations, networks, infrastructures, cultural solidarities, and modes of collaboration in order to address the totality of issues confronting society and the need to get at the roots of those injustices sapping America like an all-consuming plague.

Democratic hope poses the important challenge of how to reclaim social agency within a broader struggle to deepen the possibilities for global justice and democracy. Judith Butler is right in insisting that "there is more hope in the world when we can question what is taken for granted, especially about what it is to be human."[23] Bauman extends this insight by arguing that the resurrection of any viable notion of political and social agency is dependent upon a culture of questioning, whose purpose, as he puts it, is to "keep the forever unexhausted and unfulfilled human potential open, fighting back all attempts to foreclose and pre-empt the further unraveling of human possibilities, prodding human society to go on questioning itself and preventing that questioning from ever stalling or being declared finished."[24] The death of hope, its commodification, and its romanticization are not enough to explain the absence of struggle in the United States. Mass ignorance and indoctrination matter, as does the political economy that manufactures them, but at stake here are larger issues about those modes of education, socialization, and the production of an American public that has been successfully conditioned to comply with its own surveillance, alienation, and subjugation.

The fear of taking power has deeper roots in the American public than simply the plague of not knowing. While the pedagogical nature of politics cannot be disavowed, it must be supplemented by a deeper understanding of how capitalism subverts peoples' needs, how depth psychology works through dominant cultural and indoctrination apparatuses to atrophy the civic spirit, commercially mediate the drive for pleasure, and deter social imagination in order to deliberately deny public focus both on the possibility of social improvement and resistance to all that delays it. As such, neoliberal practices are a war waged as much against the larger economic social fabric as they are against the individual and collective psyche. And if the left and progressives are to address these elements of low-intensity cultural and financial warfare on the home front they will have to connect hope to a sustained inquiry, as Stanley Aronowitz argues, over the shaping of the political and cultural unconscious.[25]

Outrage has been deterred and redirected from political organizing and ethical community-building to self-deprecation, depression, cynicism, a fear of the other, a contempt of the disadvantaged, and a disgust for democratic solidarities. War has become a fully normalized way of life in the United States. It has been elevated to an all-encompassing ideology and politics that includes both a view of the population as potential suspects in need of constant surveillance and an aggressive intolerance of people who question authority or protest, whether they are educators, journalists, or ordinary citizens who have simply had enough. Hope provides a potential register of resistance, a new language, a different understanding of society, and a view of the future in which governing authorities are fully accountable to and compliant with the will of the public, and not the other way around. Hope also accentuates how politics might be played out on the terrain of imagination and desire as well as in material relations of power and concrete social formations. Freedom and justice, in this instance, have to be mediated through the connection between civic education and political agency, which presupposes that the goal of hope is not to liberate the individual *from* the social—a central tenet of neoliberalism—but to take seriously the notion that the individual can only be liberated *through* the social.

Democratic hope is a subversive, defiant practice that makes power visible and interrogates and resists those events, social relations, and ideas that threaten democracy and the public spheres necessary to practice it. Hope at its best provides a link, however transient, provisional, and contextual, between passion, vision, and critique, on the one hand, and engagement and transformation on the other. But for such a notion of hope to be consequential it has to be grounded in a pedagogical project that has some hold on the present. Hope becomes meaningful to the degree that it identifies agencies and processes, offers alternatives to an age of profound pessimism, reclaims an ethic of compassion and justice, and struggles for those institutions in which equality, freedom, and justice flourish as part of the ongoing networks, struggles, and solidarities for democracy everywhere.

Yet such hopes do not materialize out of thin air. They have to be nourished, developed, debated, examined, and acted upon to become meaningful. And this takes time and demands what might be called an "impatient patience." When outrage and conscience are rendered silent, crippling the mind, imagination, spirit, and collective will, it becomes almost impossible to fight the galloping forces of authoritarianism that beset the United States and many other countries. But one cannot dismiss as impossible what is simply difficult, even if such difficulty defies hope itself. Bauman is right, once again, in arguing that "as to our hopes: hope is one human quality we are bound never to lose without losing our humanity. But we may be similarly certain that a safe haven in which to drop its anchor will take a very long time to be found."[26] The future of American society lies in opposition to the surveillance state at home and its seamless connection to waging constant war and acts of aggression abroad.

State violence is not a measure of greatness and honor. Such violence trades in incredulous appeals to personal security and fear mongering in its efforts to paralyze the impulse for justice, the culture of investigation, and the courage necessary to oppose complicity with the many varieties of ongoing civic and economic mass destruction resulting from the collusion of state and corporate forces. Hope turns radical when it exposes the violence of organized forgetting—acts of state and corporate aggression against democracy, humanity, and ecological stability itself. But hope does more than critique, dismantle, and expose the ideologies, values, institutions, and social relations that are pushing so many countries today into authoritarianism, austerity, violence, and war.

Hope, driven by imagination, yearns for more than a retreat into the language of criticism. Hope can energize and mobilize groups, neighborhoods, communities, campuses, and networks of people to articulate and advance insurgent discourses in the movement toward developing an insurrectional democracy. Hope is an important political and subjective register that can not only enable people to think beyond the disimagination machine—the chronic and intergenerational injustices deeply structured into all levels of society—but also to advance forms of egalitarian community that celebrate the voice, well-being, inherent dignity, and participation of each person as an integral thread in the ever-evolving fabric of living democracy.

NOTES

INTRODUCTION

1. See, for example, Radley Balko, *Rise of the Warrior Cop: The Militarization of America's Police Forces* (New York: Public Affairs, 2013) and Chase Madar, "Everyone Is a Criminal: On the Over-Policing of America," *Huffington Post* (December 13, 2013). Online: http://www.huffingtonpost.com/chase-madar/over-policing-of-america_b_4412187.html

2. Jeremy Gilbert, "What Kind of Thing Is 'Neoliberalism'?" *New Formations* 55: 80/81 (Winter 2013), p. 9.

3. Ernst Bloch quoted in Anson Rabinach, "Unclaimed Heritage: Ernst Bloch's *Heritage of Our Times* and the Theory of Fascism," *New German Critique* (Spring 1977), p. 8; see also Richard Johnson, "Optimism of the Intellect? Hegemony and hope," *Soundings* 54 (Summer 2013), pp. 51–65.

4. Tyler Kingkade, "Mike Reynolds, Oklahoma Rep: 'It's Not Our Job to See That Anyone Gets an Education,'" *Huffington Post* (April 8, 2013). Online: http://www.huffingtonpost.com/2013/04/08/mike-reynolds-education_n_3038157.html

5. Steffie Woolhandler, "Republican State Lawmakers' Refusal to Expand Medicaid Will Result in Thousands of Deaths," *The Real News* (March 8, 2014). Online: http://therealnews.com/t2/index.php?option=com_content&task=view&id=31&Itemid=74&jumival=11415

6. Paul Bucheitt, "4 Ways the Koch Brothers' Wealth Is Beyond Comprehension," *AlterNet* (November 24, 2013). Online: http://www.alternet.org/economy/4-ways-koch-brothers-wealth-beyond-comprehension

7. Frank B. Wilderson III, "Introduction: Unspeakable Ethics," *Red, White, & Black* (London: Duke University Press, 2012), p. 2.

8. Corrie MacLaggan, "Texas Legislature Passes Measure to Prevent Medicaid Expansion," *Huffington Post* (May 27, 2013). Online: http://www.huffingtonpost.com/2013/05/27/texas-medicaid_n_3341034.html

9. Thom Hartmann Program, "Conservatives: The New Taliban," *Truthout* (March 13, 2013). Online: http://truth-out.org/opinion/item/15107-conservatives-the-new-taliban

10. Noam Chomsky, "Anti-Democratic Nature of US Capitalism Is Being Exposed," *Irish Times* (October 10, 2008). Online: http://www.commondreams.org/view/2008/10/10-4

11. Jonathan Turley, "10 Reasons the U.S. Is No Longer the Land of the Free," *Washington Post* (January 13, 2012). Online: http://articles.washingtonpost.com/2012-01-13/opinions/35440628_1_individual-rights-indefinite-detention-citizens

12. Habiba Alcindor, "Censoring Books in Arizona," *The Nation*, January 30, 2012. Accessed January 14, 2014: http://www.thenation.com/blog/165939/censoring-books-arizona#

13. Zoe Williams, "The Saturday Interview: Stuart Hall," *The Guardian* (February 11, 2012). Online: http://www.guardian.co.uk/theguardian/2012/feb/11/saturday-interview-stuart-hall

14. I have paraphrased in this sentence Kristen Case's phrase "moments of classroom grace." See Kristen Case, "The Other Public Humanities," *Chronicle of Higher Education* (January 13, 2014). Online: http://m.chronicle.com/article/Ahas-Ahead/143867

15. Ibid.

16. Ibid.

CHAPTER ONE

1. I address this issue in Henry A. Giroux, *The University in Chains: Challenging the Military-Industrial-Academic Complex* (Boulder: Paradigm, 2007).

2. There are a number of books that discuss this topic, and too many excellent texts to mention them all. A brief selection would include Patricia J. Williams, *Seeing a Color-Blind Future: The Paradox of Race* (New York: Noonday Press, 1997); David Theo Goldberg, *The Racial State* (Malden, MA: Blackwell, 2002); Eduardo Bonilla-Silva, *Racism without Racists: Color-Blind Racism and the Persistence of Racial Inequality in America* (Boulder: Rowman & Littlefield, 2009); Tim Wise, *Colorblind: The Rise of Post-Racial Politics and the Retreat from Racial Equity* (San Francisco: City Lights, 2010); Da-

vid Theo Goldberg, *The Threat of Race* (Malden: Wiley-Blackwell, 2010); Susan Searls Giroux, *Between Race and Reason: Violence, Intellectual Responsibility, and the University to Come* (Stanford: Stanford University Press, 2010); and Michelle Alexander, *The New Jim Crow: Mass Incarceration in the Age of Colorblindness* (New York: The New Press, 2010).

3. Georges Didi-Huberman, *Images in Spite of All: Four Photographs from Auschwitz*, trans. Shane B. Lillis (Chicago: University of Chicago Press, 2008), pp. 1–2.

4. Katherine Stewart, "Is Texas Waging War on History?" *AlterNet* (May 21, 2012). Online: http://www.alternet.org/story/155515/is_texas_waging_war_on_history

5. Ibid.

6. See, for instance, Chris Mooney, *The Republican Brain: The Science of Why They Deny Science and Reality* (New York: Wiley, 2012).

7. See, for instance, Anthony DiMaggio, *The Rise of the Tea Party* (New York: Monthly Review Press, 2011); Paul Street and Anthony DiMaggio, *Crashing the Tea Party* (Boulder, Paradigm, 2011); Will Bunch, *The Backlash: Right-Wing Radicals, High-Def Hucksters, and Paranoid Politics in the Age of Obama* (New York: Harper, 2010).

8. Steve Horn, "Three States Pushing ALEC Bill to Require Teachng Climate Change Denial in Schools," *Desmogblog.com* (January 31, 2013). Online: www.desmogblog.com/2013/01/31/three-states-pushing-alec-bill-climate-change-denial-schools

9. Igor Volsky, "Arizona Bill to Force Students to Take a Loyalty Oath," *AlterNet* (January 26, 2013). Online: http://www.alternet.org/arizona-bill-force-students-take-loyalty-oath

10. J. M. Coetzee, "Universites Head for Extinction," *Guardian* (November 1, 2013). Online: http://m.mg.co.za/index.php?view=article&urlid=2013-11-01-universities-head-for-extinction%2F&views=1&mobi=true&KEY=mraqm2vufth65l0hhsa0i921h1#.UtwBkNLTmt8

11. Heidi Boghosian, *Spying on Democracy: Government Surveillance, Corporate Power, and Public Resistance* (City Lights Books, 2013).

12. Personal correspondence and lecture at McMaster University on July 22, 2013.

13. Brad Evans and Julian Reid, *Resilient Life: The Art of Living Dangerously* (London: Polity, 2013).

14. Robin D. G. Kelley, "Empire State of Mind," *Counter-Punch*, (August 16, 2013). Online: http://www.counterpunch.org/2013/08/16/empire-state-of-mind

15. Alexander, *The New Jim Crow.*

16. Kate Epstein, "Total Surveillance," *CounterPunch* (June 28–30, 2013). Online: http://www.counterpunch.org/2013/06/28/total-surveillance

17. This history has been addressed by many writers. See especially, David Harvey, *A Brief History of Neoliberalism* (New York: Oxford University Press, 2005) Stuart Hall, "The Neo-Liberal Revolution," *Cultural Studies* 25: 6 (November 2011), pp. 705–728.

18. See, for instance, Charles H. Ferguson, *Predator Nation: Corporate Criminals, Political Corruption, and the Hijacking of America* (New York: Crown Business, 2013).

19. Tony Judt, *Ill Fares the Land* (New York: Penguin Press, 2010).

20. These themes are taken up in Lawrence Grossberg, *Caught in the Crossfire: Kids, Politics, and America's Future* (Boulder: Paradigm Publishers, 2005) and Henry A. Giroux, *Youth in a Suspect Society* (New York: Palgrave Macmillan, 2009).

21. I discuss this subject in a number of books. See, for example, Henry A. Giroux, *Education and the Crisis of Public Values* (New York: Peter Lang, 2012).

22. See Jean and John Comaroff, "Reflections of Youth, from the Past to the Postcolony," in *Frontiers of Capital: Ethnographic Reflections on The New Economy*, ed. Melissa S. Fisher and Greg Downey (Durham, NC: Duke University Press, 2006), pp. 267–281.

23. Michael D. Yates, "Public School Teachers: New Unions, New Alliances, New Politics," *Truthout.org* (July 24, 2013). Online: http://truth-out.org/opinion/item/17756-public-school-teachers-new-unions-new-alliances-new-politics

24. Zygmunt Bauman, *Liquid Times: Living in an Age of Uncertainty* (Cambridge: Polity Press, 2007), p. 14.

25. This collapse of the public into the private has long been

the concern of an older generation of intellectuals extending from C. Wright Mills and Hannah Arendt to Ulrich Beck and Zygmunt Bauman.

26. Zygmunt Bauman, "Downward Mobility Is Now a Reality," *Guardian* (May 31, 2012). Online: http://www.guardian.co.uk/commentisfree/2012/may/31/downward-mobility-europe-young-people. Bauman develops this theme in detail in both *On Education* (Cambridge, UK: Polity Press, 2012) and *This Is Not a Diary* (Cambridge, UK: Polity Press, 2012).

27. Zygmunt Bauman, *Wasted Lives* (London: Polity, 2004), p. 76.

28. Ibid.

29. Michael Lerner, "Trayvon Martin: A Jewish Response," *Tikkun* (July 14, 2013). Online: http://friendfeed.com/911bloggerin

30. Bauman, *On Education*, p. 47.

31. Ibid.

32. I have borrowed the term "zones of social abandonment" from João Biehl, *Vita: Life in a Zone of Social Abandonment* (Berkeley: University of California Press, 2005). See also Henry A. Giroux, *Disposable Youth* (New York: Routledge, 2012) and Alexander, *The New Jim Crow*.

33. Angela Y. Davis, "State of Emergency," in *Racializing Justice, Disenfranchising Lives*, ed. Manning Marable, Keesha Middlemass, and Ian Steinberg (New York: Palgrave, 2007), p. 324.

34. Hardt and Negri, *Declaration*, p. 20.

35. Ibid.

36. See Loic Wacquant, *Punishing the Poor: The Neoliberal Government of Social Insecurity* (Durham, NC: Duke University Press, 2009).

37. Kate Epstein, "Total Surveillance," *CounterPunch*, (June 28–30, 2013). Online: http://www.counterpunch.org/2013/06/28/total-surveillance

38. John Steppling, "Control & Punish," *JohnSteppling.com* (June 22, 2013). Online: http://john-steppling.com/control-punish

39. Kyle Bella, "Bodies in Alliance: Gender Theorist Judith Butler on the Occupy and SlutWalk Movements," *Truthout* (December

15, 2011). Online: http://www.truth-out.org/bodies-alliance-gender-theorist-judith-butler-occupy-and-slutwalk-movements/1323880210

40. I take this up in Giroux, *Education and the Crisis of Public Values*.

41. Published documentation of each and every of these arrests is published on this website: http://stpeteforpeace.org/occupyarrests.sources.html

42. Adam Gopnik, "The Caging of America," *New Yorker* (January 30, 2012). Online: http://www.newyorker.com/arts/critics/atlarge/2012/01/30/120130crat_atlarge_gopnik

43. Stuart Hall cited in James Hay, "Interview with Stuart Hall," *Communication and Critical/Cultural Studies* 10: 1 (2013), pp. 10–33.

44. Hardt and Negri, *Declaration*, p. 23.

45. There are many sources that address this issue. See, in particular, Melvin A. Goodman, *National Insecurity: The Cost of American Militarism* (San Francisco: City Lights, 2013).

46. Hall, "The Neo-Liberal Revolution," p. 706.

47. Daniel Bell, *The End of Ideology: On the Exhaustion of Political Ideas in the Fifties* (New York: Free Press, 1966) and the more recent Francis Fukuyama, *The End of History and the Last Man* (New York: Free Press, 2006).

48. Stuart Hall, "The March of the Neoliberals," *Guardian* (September 12, 2011). Online: http://www.guardian.co.uk/politics/2011/sep/12/march-of-the-neoliberals

49. Alex Honneth, *Pathologies of Reason* (New York: Columbia University Press, 2009), p. 188.

50. C. Wright Mills, *The Power Elite* (New York: Oxford University Press, 2000), p. 222.

51. See Gore Vidal, *Perpetual War for Perpetual Peace* (New York: Nation Books, 2002); Gore Vidal, *Imperial America: Reflections on the United States of Amnesia* (New York: Nation Books, 2004); Chris Hedges, *War Is a Force That Gives Us Meaning* (New York: Anchor Books, 2003); Chalmers Johnson, *The Sorrows of Empire: Militarism, Secrecy, and the End of the Republic* (New York: Metropolitan Books, 2004); Andrew Bacevich, *The New American Militarism* (New York: Oxford University Press, 2005); Chalmers Johnson, *Nemesis: The Last*

Days of the Republic (Henry Holt, 2006); Nick Turse, *The Complex: How the Military Invades Our Everyday Lives* (New York: Metropolitan Books, 2008); and Andrew J. Bacevich, *Washington Rules: America's Path to Permanent War* (New York: Metropolitan Books, 2010).

52. On the nature of permanent war, see Gregory D. Johnson, "60 Words and a War without End: The Untold Story of the Most Dangerous Sentence in U.S. History," *BuzzFeed* (January 16, 2014). Online: http://www.buzzfeed.com/gregorydjohnsen/60-words-and-a-war-without-end-the-untold-story-of-the-most

53. Hardt and Negri, *Declaration*, p. 22.

54. Andrew Becker and G.W. Schulz, "Cops Ready for War," *Reader Supported News* (December 21, 2011). Online: http://reader-supportednews.org/news-section2/316-20/9023-focus-cops-ready-for-war

55. Ibid.

56. Glenn Greenwald, "The Roots of the UC-Davis Pepper-Spraying," *Salon* (Nov. 20, 2011). Online: http://www.salon.com/2011/11/20/the_roots_of_the_uc_davis_pepper_spraying/

57. Erica Goode, "Many in U.S. Are Arrested by Age 23, Study Finds," *New York Times* (December 19, 2011), p. A15.

58. Alexander, *The New Jim Crow*.

59. Michael Geyer, "The Militarization of Europe, 1914–1945," in *The Militarization of the Western World*, ed. John R. Gillis (New York: Rutgers University Press, 1989), p. 79.

60. Tony Judt, "The New World Order," *New York Review of Books* 11: 2 (July 14, 2005), p. 17.

61. David Graeber, "Dead Zones of the Imagination," *HAU: Journal of Ethnographic Theory* 2 (2012), p. 115.

62. Jenna Wortham, "Stealth Wear Aims to Make a Tech Statement," *New York Times* (June 29, 2013). Online: http://www.nytimes.com/2013/06/30/technology/stealth-wear-aims-to-make-a-tech-statement.html?_r=0

63. Steve Herbert and Elizabeth Brown, "Conceptions of Space and Crime in the Punitive Neoliberal City," *Antipode* (2006), p. 757.

64. Rod Bastanmehr, "Absurd: Billionaire Koch Brother Claims

Eliminating Minimum Wage Would Help the Poor," *AlterNet* (July 11, 2013). Online: http://www.alternet.org/print/news-amp-politics/ absurd-billionaire-koch-brother-claims-eliminating-minimum-wage-would-help-poor

65. Hannah Groch-Begley, "Fox Asks if Children Should Work for School Meals," *Media Matters* (April 25, 2013). Online: http://mediamatters.org/blog/2013/04/25/ fox-asks-if-children-should-work-for-school-mea/193768

66. Amanda Terkel, "Maine GOP Legislators Looking to Loosen Child Labour Laws," *Huffington Post* (March 30, 2011). Online: http://www.huffingtonpost.com/2011/03/30/maine-gop-legislators-loo_n_842563.html

67. Pascale-Anne Brault and Michael Naas, "Translators' Note," in Jean-Luc Nancy, *The Truth of Democracy* (New York: Fordham University Press, 2010), p. ix.

68. Katrina vanden Heuvel, "The Appalling GOP," *Washington Post* (July 16, 2013). Online: http://articles.washingtonpost. com/2013-07-16/opinions/40599899_1_congressional-republicans-food-stamps-legislation

69. Paul Krugman, "From the Mouths of Babes," *New York Times* (May 30, 2013). Online: http://www.nytimes.com/2013/05/31/ opinion/from-the-mouths-of-babes.html

70. Jason Deparle and Robert M. Gebeloff, "Living on Nothing but Food Stamps," *New York Times* (January 3, 2010), p. A1.

71. Alexander, *The New Jim Crow*.

72. Alex Kane, "Diabetic High School Girl Beaten by Police Officer and Arrested – for Falling Asleep in Class," *AlterNet* (May 7, 2013). Online: http://www.alternet.org/news-amp-politics/ diabetic-high-school-girl-beaten-police-officer-and-arrested-falling-asleep-class. Jordana Ossad, "Parents: Bronx Boy Handcuffed over $5 Theft," *CNN* (January 31, 2013). Online: http://www.cnn. com/2013/01/30/justice/new-york-bronx-boy-handcuff

73. Joaquin Sapien, "Texas Students Thrown in Jail for Days . . . as Punishment for Missing School?" *AlterNet* (June 13, 2013). Online: http://www.alternet.org/texas-truancy

74. Jenna Johnson, "Pledge of Allegiance Dispute Results in

Md. Teacher Having to Apologize," *Washington Post* (February 24, 2010). Online: http://www.washingtonpost.com/wp-dyn/content/article/2010/02/23/AR2010022303889.html

75. "A Failure of Imagination," *Smartypants* [blog] (March 3, 2010). Online: http://immasmartypants.blogspot.com/2010/03/failure-of-imagination.html

76. Jody Sokolower, "Schools and the New Jim Crow: An Interview with Michelle Alexander," *Truthout* (June 4, 2013). Online: http://www.truth-out.org/news/item/16756-schools-and-the-new-jim-crow-an-interview-with-michelle-alexander

77. Alexander, *The New Jim Crow*, p. 9.

78. For a particularly egregious and offensive defense of this racist stereotype, see Richard Cohen, "Racism versus Reality," *Washington Post* (July 16, 2013). Online: http://www.washingtonpost.com/opinions/richard-cohen-racism-vs-reality/2013/07/15/4f419eb6-ed7a-11e2-a1f9-ea873b7e0424_story.html?tid=pm_opinions_pop

79. Don Hazen, "The 4 Plagues: Getting a Handle on the Coming Apocalypse," *AlterNet* (June 4, 2013). Online: http://www.alternet.org/economy/4-plagues-getting-handle-coming-apocalypse

80. Gretchen Morgenson, "A Loan Fraud War That's Short on Combat," *New York Times*, March 15, 2014. Online: http://www.nytimes.com/2014/03/16/business/a-loan-fraud-war-thats-short-on-combat.html?ref=business.

81. David Price, "Memory's Half-life: A Social History of Wiretaps," *CounterPunch* 20:6 (June 2013), p. 14.

82. I discuss this issue in detail in Henry A. Giroux, *The Educational Deficit and the War on Youth* (New York: Monthly Review Press, 2013).

83. John Van Houdt, "The Crisis of Negation: An Interview with Alain Badiou," *Continent* 1: 4 (2011): 234–238. Online: http://continentcontinent.cc/index.php/continent/article/viewArticle/65

CHAPTER TWO

1. C. Wright Mills, "The Powerless People: The Role of the Intellectual in Society" in C. Wright Mills, *The Politics of Truth: Selected Writings of C. Wright Mills* (New York: Oxford University Press, 2008), p. 18.

2. Ibid. For some insightful analyses of the new authoritarianism, see Sheldon S. Wolin, *Democracy Incorporated: Managed Democracy and the Specter of Inverted Totalitarianism* (Princeton University Press, 2008); Chris Hedges, *American Fascists: The Christian Right and the War on America* (New York: Free Press, 2008); Andrew J. Bacevich, *The New American Militarism* (New York: Oxford University Press, 2005); Michael Hardt and Antonio Negri, *Multitude: War and Democracy in the Age of Empire* (New York: Penguin Press, 2004).

3. See Zygmunt Bauman, *On Education* (Cambridge, UK: Polity Press, 2012), p. 35.

4. Gerald Epstein, "Rich Should be Happy with Cliff Deal," *The Real News* (January 3, 2013). Online: http://therealnews.com/t2/index.php?option=com_content&task=view&id=31&Itemid=74&jumival=9453

5. C. Wright Mills, "Culture and Politics: The Fourth Epoch," in C. Wright Mills, *The Politics of Truth: Selected Writings of C. Wright Mills* (New York: Oxford University Press, 2008), p. 201.

6. Arundhati Roy, "What Have We Done to Democracy?" *Huffington Post* (September 27, 2009). Online at: http://www.huffingtonpost.com/arundhati-roy/what-have-we-done-to-demo_b_301294.html

7. I have borrowed this idea from Roberto Esposito, *Terms of the Political: Community, Immunity, Biopolitics* (Fordham: Fordham University Press, 2013), pp. 100–110.

8. Robert Reich, "Inequality Is Undermining Our Democracy," *Reader Supported News* (December 11, 2012). Online: http://readersupportednews.org/opinion2/279-82/14967-inequality-is-undermining-our-democracy

9. Thomas E. Mann and Norman J. Ornstein, "Let's Just Say It: The Republicans Are the Problem," *Washington Post* (April 27, 2012). Online: http://articles.washingtonpost.com/2012-04-27/opinions/35453898_1_republican-party-party-moves-democratic-party

10. Robert F. Kennedy Jr., "A Hostile Takeover of Our Country," *Reader Supported News* (October 29, 2012). Online: http://readersupportednews.org/opinion2/277-75/14252-a-hostile-takeover-of-our-country

11. Richard D. Wolff, "Fiscal Cliff Follies: Political Theater Distracts from Key Problems with the Fix," *Truthout* (January 3, 2013). Online: http://truth-out.org/opinion/item/13685-fiscal-cliff-follies-political-theater-distracts-from-ky-problems-with-the-fix

12. For the most extensive and exhaustive history on the technology of torture, see Darius Rejali, *Torture and Democracy* (Princeton: Princeton University Press, 2007). Some of the more instructive books on torture under the George W. Bush administration include Mark Danner, *Torture and Truth: America, Abu Ghraib, and the War on Terror* (New York: New York Review of Books, 2004); Jane Mayer, *The Dark Side: The Inside Story of How the War on Terror Turned into a War on American Ideals* (New York: Doubleday, 2008); and Philippe Sands, *Torture Team* (London: Penguin, 2009). On the torture of children, see Michael Haas, *George W. Bush, War Criminal? The Bush Administration's Liability for 269 War Crimes* (Westport: Praeger, 2009). See also Alex Kane, "5 Ways President Obama Has Doubled Down on Bush's Most Tragic Mistakes," *AlterNet* (January 8, 2103), online: http://www.alternet.org/civil-liberties/5-ways-president-obama-has-doubled-down-bushs-most-tragic-mistakes; and Salvatore Babones, "There Is No American Left," *Truthout* (December 27, 2012), online: http://truth-out.org/opinion/item/13567-there-is-no-american-left

13. Glenn Greenwald, "Extremism Normalized: How Americans Now Acquiesce to Once Unthinkable Ideas," *Salon* (July 31, 2012). Online: http://www.salon.com/2012/07/31/extremism_normalized

14. Robert W. McChesney, "This Isn't What Democracy Looks like," *Monthly Review* 64: 6 (2012), p. 2.

15. Michael Hudson, "The Financial Elite's War against the US Economy," *CommonDreams* (December 31, 2012). Online: https://www.commondreams.org/view/2012/12/31-8

16. George Lakoff and Glenn W. Smith, "Romney, Ryan and the Devil's Budget," *Reader Supported News* (August 22, 2012). Online: http://blogs.berkeley.edu/2012/08/23/romney-ryan-and-the-devils-budget-will-america-keep-its-soul/

17. "75 Economic Numbers from 2012 That Are Almost Too Crazy to Believe," *The Economic Collapse Blog* (December 20, 2012).

Online: http://theeconomiccollapseblog.com/archives/75-economic-numbers-from-2012-that-are-almost-too-crazy-to-believe

18. All of these quotes come from John Clarke, "Subordinating the Social? Neoliberalism and the Remaking of Welfare Capitalism," *Cultural Studies* 21: 6 (November 2007), pp. 974–987. See also John Clarke, "Governing the Social?," *Cultural Studies* 21: 6 (November 2007), p. 996.

19. Zygmunt Bauman, *This Is Not a Diary* (Cambridge: Polity Press, 2012), pp. 86–87.

20. Clarke, "Subordinating the Social?," p. 977.

21. Manfred B. Steger and Ravi K. Roy, *Neoliberalism: A Very Short Introduction* (New York: Oxford University Press, 2010), pp. 2–3.

22. Mike Davis and Daniel Bertrand Monk, "Introduction," in Mike Davis and Daniel Bertrand Monk, eds., *Evil Paradises* (New York: The New Press, 2007), p. x.

23. Tony Judt, *Ill Fares the Land* (New York: Penguin Press, 2010)

24. Zygmunt Bauman, *On Education* (Cambridge: Polity Press, 2012), p. 129.

25. Robert O. Self, "The Antisocial Contract," *New York Times* (August 25, 2012). Online: http://campaignstops.blogs.nytimes.com/2012/08/25/the-antisocial-contract/

26. Tony Judt, "I Am Not Pessimistic in the Very Long Run," *The Independent* (March 24, 2010). Online: http://www.independent.co.uk/arts-entertainment/books/features/tony-judt-i-am-not-pessimistic-in-the-very-long-run-1925966.html

27. Ibid.

28. Edward Said is particularly helpful on this issue. See, for instance, *Representations of the Intellectual* (New York: Vintage, 1996) and *Humanism and Democratic Criticism* (New York: Columbia University Press, 2004).

29. Cornelius Castoriadis, "The Problem of Democracy Today," *Democracy and Nature*, 8 (April 1996), pp. 18–35.

30. Cornelius Castoriadis, "Democracy as Procedure and Democracy as Regime," *Constellations* 4: 1 (1997), p. 10.

31. Gayatri Chakravorty Spivak, "'Changing Reflexes': Interview with Gayatri Chakravorty Spivak," *Works and Days* 28: 55/56 (2010), p. 2.

32. Zygmunt Bauman, *Does Ethics Have a Chance in a World of Consumers?* (Cambridge: Harvard University Press, 2008), p. 73.

33. Jacques Derrida, "The Future of the Profession or the Unconditional University," in Laurence Simmons and Heather Worth, eds., *Derrida Downunder* (Auckland: Dunmore Press, 2001), p. 7.

34. A Conversation between Lani Guinier and Anna Deavere Smith, "Rethinking Power, Rethinking Theater," *Theater* 31: 3 (Winter 2002), p. 3.

35. Ibid.

36. Theodor W. Adorno, *Critical Models: Interventions and Catchwords* (New York: Columbia University Press, 2005), pp. 291–292.

37. Robert Hass cited in Sarah Pollock, "Robert Hass," *Mother Jones* (March/April 1992), p. 22.

38. Richard Swift, *The No-Nonsense Guide to Democracy* (Toronto: Between the Lines, 2002), p. 138.

39. Alain Badiou, *Ethics: An Essay on the Understanding of Evil* (London: Verso, 1998), p. 116.

CHAPTER THREE

1. Zygmunt Bauman, *This Is Not a Diary* (Cambridge: Polity, 2012), p. 18.

2. On the politics of disposability, see João Biehl, *Vita: Life in A Zone of Social Abandonment* (Los Angeles: University of California Press, 2005); Zygmunt Bauman, *Wasted Lives* (London: Polity Press, 2004); Henry A. Giroux, *Stormy Weather: Katrina and the Politics of Disposability* (Boulder, Paradigm, 2006); Judith Butler, *Precarious Life: The Powers of Mourning and Violence* (London: Verso Press, 2004); and Achille Mbembe, "Necropolitics," trans. by Libby Meintjes, *Public Culture* 15: 1 (2003), pp. 11–40.

3. A number of important books have addressed the financial crisis. Some recent examples include Jeff Marrick, *The Age of Greed: The Triumph of Finance and the Decline of America, 1970 to the Present* (New York: Vintage, 2011); John Bellamy Foster and Robert W.

McChesney, *The Endless Crisis: How Monopoly-Finance Capital Produces Stagnation and Upheaval from the USA to China* (New York: Monthly Review Press, 2012); Charles H. Ferguson, *Predator Nation: Corporate Criminals, Political Corruption, and the Hijacking of America* (New York: Crown Publishing, 2012); Christopher Hayes, *Twilight of Elites: America after Meritocracy* (New York: Crown Publishing, 2012); and Richard Wolff, *Occupy the Economy: Challenging Capitalism* (San Francisco: City Lights, 2012).

4. Naomi Klein has written an important account of how contemporary capitalism uses natural disasters to pave the way for free-market enterprise in *The Shock Doctrine: The Rise of Disaster Capitalism* (New York: Knopf, 2007).

5. Gretchen Morgenson, "A Loan Fraud War That's Short on Combat," *New York Times*, (March 15, 2014). Online: http://nyti.ms/1fzqhcJ

6. Ibid.

7. Chase Madar, "Everyone Is a Criminal: On the Over-Policing of America", *Huffington Post* (December 13, 2013). Online: http://www.huffingtonpost.com/chase-madar/over-policing-of-america_b_4412187.html

8. Nick Pinto, "Hurricane Sandy Is New York's Katrina," *Village Voice* (November 21, 2012). Online: http://www.villagevoice.com/2012-11-21/news/hurricane-sandy-is-new-york-s-katrina

9. Some recent sources on the politics of inequality include Joseph Stiglitz, *The Politics of Inequality* (New York: Norton, 2012) and Richard Wilkinson and Kate Pickett, *The Spirit Level: Why Equality Is Better for Everyone* (New York: Penguin Press, 2010).

10. Paul Buchheit, "Five Misconceptions about Our Tattered Safety Net," *Common Dreams* (November 12, 2012). Online: http://www.commondreams.org/view/2012/11/12

11. Joseph E. Stiglitz, "The Price of Inequality," *Project Syndicate* (June 5, 2012). Online: http://www.project-syndicate.org/commentary/the-price-of-inequality

12. VOA News, "Oxfam: 85 Wealthiest People Own as Much as Half the World's Population," *Voice of America* (January 21, 2014). Online: http://www.voanews.com/articleprintview/1834791.html

13. Sarah Seltzer, "Hurricane Sandy: Income Inequality Writ Large," *Salon* (November 1, 2012). Online: http://www.salon.com/2012/11/01/hurricane_sandy_a_portrait_of_income_inequality

14. Nina Bernstein, "Storm Bared a Lack of Options for the Homeless in New York," *New York Times* (November 20, 2012), p. A1.

15. Andrea Elliott and Rebecca R. Ruiz, "New York Is Removing Over 400 Children From 2 Homeless Shelters," *New York Times*, February 21, 2014. Online: http://www.nytimes.com/2014/02/21/nyregion/new-york-is-removing-over-400-children-from-2-homeless-shelters.html

16. Sarah Seltzer, "Hurricane Sandy."

17. Teddy Cruz, "Democratizing Urbanization and the Search for a New Civic Imagination," in *Living as Form: Socially Engaged Art from 1991-2011*, ed. Nato Thompson (Cambridge, Mass.: MIT Press, 2012), p. 58.

18. Naomi Klein, "Superstorm Sandy - A People's Shock?" *The Nation* (November 5, 2012). Online: http://www.thenation.com/article/171048/superstorm-sandy-peoples-shock

19. David Rohde, "The Hideous Inequality Exposed by Hurricane Sandy," *The Atlantic* (October 31, 2012). Online: http://www.theatlantic.com/business/archive/2012/10/the-hideous-inequality-exposed-by-hurricane-sandy/264337

20. David B. Caruso, "Sick, Frail Struggle Most in Storm's Aftermath," *Associated Press* (November 10, 2012). Online: http://www.waff.com/story/20060243/drivers-grapple-with-nyc-gas-rationing-after-sandy

21. John Leslie, "After Sandy: Political Storm Coming?" *Socialist Organizer* (November 5, 2012). Online: http://socialistorganizer.org/after-sandy-political-storm-coming

22. Rohde, "Hideous Inequality Exposed."

23. Ibid.

24. Editor, "Hurricane Sandy's Lesson: Profit System Breeds Disaster," *Workers World* (November 7, 2012). Online: http://www.workers.org/2012/11/07/hurricane-sandys-lesson-profit-system-breeds-disaster

25. Joseph Stiglitz, "Politics Is at the Root of the Problem," *Eu-*

ropean Magazine (April 23, 2012). Online: http://theeuropean-magazine.com/633-stiglitz-joseph/634-austerity-and-a-new-recession

26. Adam Gabatt, "House Delay over $60BN Sandy Aid Bill Prompts Anger and Outrage," *Guardian* (January 2, 2013), online: http://www.guardian.co.uk/world/2013/jan/02/house-delay-sandy-aid-bill-anger; and Raymond Hernandez, "Stalling of Storm Aid Makes Northeast Republicans Furious," *New York Times* (January 2, 2013), online: http://www.nytimes.com/2013/01/03/nyregion/congressional-members-blast-house-for-ignoring-storm-aid-bill.html?nl=todaysheadlines&emc=edit_th_20130103&_r=0

27. Etienne Balibar, "Outline of a Topography of Cruelty: Citizenship and Civility in the Era of Global Violence," in *We, the People of Europe? Reflections on Transnational Citizenship* (Princeton: Princeton University Press, 2004), p. 128.

28. See, for example, Larry M. Bartels, *Unequal Democracy: The Political Economy of the New Gilded Age* (Princeton: Princeton University Press, 2008); John K. Galbraith, *The Predator State* (New York: Free Press, 2008); Jacob S. Hacker and Paul Pierson, *Winner-Take-All Politics: How Washington Made the Richer Richer—And Turned Its Back on the Middle Class* (New York: Simon and Schuster, 2010); and Juliet B. Schor, *Plenitude: The New Economics of True Wealth* (New York: Penguin Press, 2010).

29. Bauman, *Wasted Lives*, p. 76.

30. Paul Krugman, "Plutocrats Feeling Persecuted," *New York Times*, September 26, 2013. Online: http://www.nytimes.com/2013/09/27/opinion/krugman-plutocrats-feeling-persecuted.html?_r=0

31. Mariana Garces and Steve Rendall, "Media Not Concerned about the Very Poor," *Fair: Fairness in Accuracy and Reporting* (September 2012). Online: http://www.fair.org/index.php?page=4604

32. Ibid.

33. Corn, "Secret Video," http://www.motherjones.com/politics/2012/09/secret-video-romney-private-fundraiser

34. Ashley Parker, "Romney Blames Loss on Obama's 'Gifts' to Minorities and Young Voters," *New York Times* (November 14, 2012), p. A23.

35. Nsenga K. Burton, "Obama Has Not Undermined Welfare Reform," *Star Telegram* (September 19, 2012). Online: http://www. star-telegram.com/2012/09/19/4272639/obama-has-not-under-mined-welfare.html

36. Cited in Amy Goodman, "Tavis Smiley, Cornel West on the 2012 Election and Why Calling Obama 'Progressive' Ignores His Record," *Democracy Now* (November 9, 2012). Online: http://www. democracynow.org/2012/11/9/tavis_smiley_cornel_west_on_the

37. Alex Koppelman, "The Marathon Is Cancelled—Finally," *The New Yorker* (November 2, 2012). Online: http://www.newyorker. com/online/blogs/newsdesk/2012/11/marathon-is-cancelled-finally. html

38. Alan Woods, "USA: After the Storm—The Mood Turns Angry," *In Defence of Marxism* (November 5, 2012). Online: http://www. marxist.com/after-the-storm-the-mood-turns-angry.htm

39. Chris Hedges, "Elites Will Make Gazans of Us All," *Truth-dig* (November 19, 2012). Online: http://www.truthdig.com/report/item/elites_will_make_gazans_of_us_all_20121119

40. Cited in Klein, "Superstorm Sandy."

41. Editorial "A Big Storm Requires Big Government," *New York Times* (October 29, 2012). Online: http://www.nytimes. com/2012/10/30/opinion/a-big-storm-requires-big-government. html?_r=0. See also Joan Walsh, "Mitt Blows It on Sandy: Did the Hurricane Just Cost Him the Election?" *AlterNet* (October 31, 2012). Online: http://www.alternet.org/election-2012/mitt-blows-it-sandy-did-hurricane-just-cost-him-election

42. Chris Hedges and Joe Sacco, *Days of Destruction, Days of Revolt* (Toronto: Knopf Canada, 2012).

43. Bill Moyer Interviews Chris Hedges, "Capitalism's 'Sacrifice Zones,'" *Moyers & Company* (July 20, 2012). Online: http://billmoyers.com/wp-content/themes/billmoyers/transcript-print. php?post=10998

44. Danny Weil, "Film 'Won't Back Down' Models Hollywood Propaganda in Age of School Reform," *Truthout* (September 5, 2012). Online: http://truth-out.org/news/item/11225-film-wont-back-down-models-hollywood-propaganda-in-age-of-school-reform

45. Garry Wills, "Our Moloch," *New York Review* (December 15, 2012). Online: http://www.nybooks.com/blogs/nyrblog/2012/dec/15/our-moloch. See also, Frank Rich, "Frank Rich: America's Other Original Sin," *New York Magazine* (December 17, 2012). Online: http://nymag.com/daily/intelligencer/2012/12/frank-rich-americas-other-original-sin.html

46. Jeff Sparrow, "When the Burning Moment Breaks: Gun Control and Rage Massacres," *Overland* (August 6, 2012). Online: http://overland.org.au/blogs/new-words/2012/08/when-the-burning-moment-breaks-gun-control-and-rage-massacres/

47. Henry A. Giroux, *Twilight of the Social: Resurgent Publics in the Age of Disposability* (Boulder: Paradigm Publishers, 2012).

48. Sarah Maslin Nir, "Helping Hands Also Expose a New York Divide," *New York Times* (November 16, 2012), p. A1.

49. Ibid.

50. Ibid.

51. Wilderson III, "Introduction: Unspeakable Ethics," p. 2.

52. See Jacques Rancière, *Hatred of Democracy* (London: Verso, 2006); and Jean-Luc Nancy, *The Truth of Democracy*, translated by Pascale-Anne Brault and Micheal Naas, (New York: Fordham University Press, 2010). For a superb analysis of the roots of democracy, see John Keane, *The Life and Death of Democracy* (New York: Norton, 2009).

53. Michael J. Sandel, *What Money Can't Buy: The Moral Limits of Markets* (New York: Farrar, Straus and Giroux, 2012), p. 6.

54. Jonathan Simon, *Governing through Crime: How the War on Crime Transformed American Democracy and Created a Culture of Fear* (New York: Oxford University Press, 2007), p. 180.

55. Slavoj Zizek, "Today, Iraq. Tomorrow . . . Democracy?" *In These Times* (March 18, 2003), p. 3.

56. See, for instance, Michelle Alexander, *The New Jim Crow: Mass Incarceration in the Age of Colorblindness* (New York: The New Press, 2010); Angela Y. Davis, *Abolition Democracy: Beyond Empire, Prisons, and Torture* (New York: Seven Stories Press, 2005); Joe Soss, Richard C. Fording, and Sanford F. Schram, *Disciplining the Poor: Neoliberal Paternalism and the Persistent Power of Race* (Chicago: Uni-

versity of Chicago Press, 2011); and Loic Wacquant, *Punishing the Poor: The Neoliberal Government of Social Insecurity* (Durham: Duke University Press, 2009).

57. Brent Staples, "California Horror Stories and the 3-Strikes Law," *New York Times* (November 25, 2012), p. SR10.

58. Robert Jay Lifton, *Death in Life: Survivors of Hiroshima* (Chapel Hill: University of North Carolina Press, 1987), p. 479. See Lynn Worsham's brilliant use of Lifton's work in her "Thinking with Cats (More to Follow)," *JAC* 30: 3-4 (2010), pp. 405–433.

59. See Tony Judt, *Ill Fares the Land* (New York: Penguin, 2010).

60. Joseph E. Stiglitz, "The Ideological Crisis of Western Capitalism," *Project Syndicate* (July 6, 2011). Online: http://www.project-syndicate.org/commentary/the-ideological-crisis-of-western-capitalism

61. Zygmunt Bauman, *In Search of Politics* (Stanford: Stanford University Press, 1999), p. 3. One example of Bauman's claim can be seen in a widely read *New York Times* article titled "Is This the End?" by James Atlas. Atlas not only ignores the pressing social and economic problems that tragically impacted many poor residents along the East Coast, but also treats the issue of climate change through a series of literary references that utterly depoliticizes the issue. This view represents the growing ecological threat to the planet as just another historical instance among many through which to contemplate our ephemerality. Matters of politics and power do more than disappear in this analysis: they collapse into a cynicism that hides behind an aestheticism that is as crude as it is barbaric. See James Atlas, "Is This the End?" *New York Times* (November 25, 2012), pp. SR 1, 7.

62. See, for example, Manuel Castells, *Networks of Outrage and Hope: Social Movements in the Internet Age* (Cambridge, Polity Press, 2012); Noam Chomsky, *Occupy* (New York: Succotti Park Press, 2012); Henry A. Giroux, *Youth in Revolt: Reclaiming a Democratic Future* (Boulder: Paradigm Publishers, 2013); and Wolff, *Occupy the Economy*.

63. Cruz, "Democratizing Urbanization."

64. Zygmunt Bauman, *Living on Borrowed Time: Conversations with Citlali Rovirosa-Madrazo* (Cambridge: Polity Press, 2010), pp.

6–7.

65. John Van Houdt, "The Crisis of Negation: An Interview with Alain Badiou," *Continent* 1: 4 (2011): 234–238.

66. On this issue, see, in particular, Leo Lowenthal, "Atomization of Man," *False Prophets: Studies in Authoritarianism* (New Brunswick: Transaction Books, 1987), pp. 181–91; and Butler, *Precarious Life*.

67. Klein, "Superstorm Sandy."

68. Tony Judt, "I Am Not Pessimistic in the Very Long Run," *The Independent* (March 24, 2010). Online: http://www.independent. co.uk/arts-entertainment/books/features/tony-judt-i-am-not-pessi-mistic-in-the-very-long-run-1925966.html

69. Tony Judt, "Transformations of the Public Sphere," *Social Science Research Council* (December 22, 2011). Online: http://public-sphere.ssrc.org/judt-the-disintegration-of-the-public-sector/

70. Ibid.

71. Ibid.

72. Dorothy Roberts, *Fatal Intervention: How Science Politics, and Big Business Re-Create Race in the Twenty-First Century* (New York: The Free Press, 2011), p. 312.

73. Ibid.

74. Ibid.

75. Butler, *Precarious Life*, pp. 33–34.

CHAPTER FOUR

1. Spencer Ackerman, "More Than 50 Countries Helped the CIA Outsource Torture," *Wired* (February 5, 2013). Online: http://www.wired.com/dangerroom/2013/02/54-countries-rendition/

2. Amrit Singh, *Globalizing Torture: CIA Secret Detention and Extraordinary Rendition* (New York: Open Society Foundation, 2013). Online: http://www.opensocietyfoundations.org/sites/default/files/globalizing-torture-20120205.pdf

3. Steve Coll, "Why *Zero Dark Thirty* Fails," *New York Review of Books* (February 7, 2013), pp. 4–6.

4. Rustom Bharacuha, "Around Adohya: Aberrations, Enigmas, and Moments of Violence," *Third Text* (Autumn 1993), p. 45.

5. Fabiola Salek and Fabiola Fernandez Salek, eds., *Screening*

Torture: Media Representations of State Terror and Political Domination (New York: Columbia University Press, 2012).

6. Michael Halberstam, *Totalitarianism and the Modern Conception of Politics* (New Haven: Yale University Press, 1999), p. 6.

7. The White Paper is cited with an online reference in Michael Isikoff, "Justice Department memo reveals legal case for drone strikes on Americans." NBC News (February 4, 2013). http://investigations. nbcnews.com/_news/2013/02/04/16843014-justice-department-memo-reveals-legal-case-for-drone-strikes-on-americans?lite

8. Singh, *Globalizing Torture*. Also see Amrit Singh, "Globalizing Torture: Ahead of Brennan Hearing, International Complicity in CIA Rendition Exposed," *Democracy Now* (February 7, 2013). Online: http://www.democracynow.org/2013/2/7/globalizing_torture_ahead_of_brennan_hearing

9. For some insightful critiques of this document, see interview with Jameel Jaffer, "Kill List Exposed: Leaked Obama Memo Shows Assassination of U.S. Citizens 'Has No Geographic Limit,'" *Democracy Now* (February 5, 2013). Online: http://www.democracynow.org/2013/2/5/kill_list_exposed_leaked_obama_memo. See also Jameel Jaffer, "The Justice Department's White Paper on Targeted Killing," *ACLU* (February 4, 2013), online: http://www. aclu.org/blog/national-security/justice-departments-white-paper-targeted-killing; Glenn Greenwald, "Chilling Legal Memo from Obama DOJ Justifies Assassination of US Citizens," *Guardian* (February 5, 2013), online: http://www.guardian.co.uk/commentis-free/2013/feb/05/obama-kill-list-doj-memo; Juan Cole, "Top Five Objections to the White House's Drone Killing Memo," *Reader Supported News* (February 6, 2013), online: http://readersupport-ednews.org/opinion2/277-75/15901-focus-top-five-objections-to-the-white-houses-drone-killing-memo; and Dennis Bernstein, "An Interview with Legal Scholar Marjorie Cohn: Why Targeted Assassinations Violate US and International Law," *CounterPunch* (February 8, 2013), online: http://www.counterpunch.org/2013/02/08/why-targeted-assassinations-violate-us-and-international-law

10. As Jameel Jaffer points out, "Without saying so explicitly, the government claims the authority to kill American terrorism suspects

in secret." See Jaffer, "The Justice Department's White Paper on Targeted Killing."

11. Greenwald, "Chilling Legal Memo."

12. Isabel Hilton, "The 800lb Gorilla in American Foreign Policy," *Guardian* (July 28, 2004). Online: http://www.guardian.co.uk/print/0,3858,4980261-103390,00.html

13. Chris McGreal, "White House to Release Legal Rationale for Killing of US Citizens with Drones," *Guardian* (February 4, 2013). Online: http://www.guardian.co.uk/world/2013/feb/07/white-house-drones

14. Interview with Jameel Jaffer, "Kill List Exposed."

15. Maria Pia Lara, *Narrating Evil: A Postmetaphysical Theory of Reflective Judgement* (NewYork: Columbia University Press, 2007), pp. 14–16, 19.

16. Roy Eidelson, "How Americans Think about Torture—and Why," *TruthOut* (May 11, 2009). Online: http://www.truthout.org/051209c

17. Frank Rich, "America Yawns at Obama's Assassination Policy," *New York Magazine* (February 7, 2012). Online: http://nymag.com/daily/intelligencer/2013/02/america-yawns-at-obamas-assassination-policy.html

18. Morris Berman, "The Moral Order" *CounterPunch* (February 8, 2013). Online: http://www.counterpunch.org/2013/02/08/the-moral-order

19. Frank B. Wilderson III, "Introduction: Unspeakable Ethics," *Red, White, & Black* (London: Duke University Press, 2012), pp. 1–32.

20. See, for example, the editorial, "To Kill An American," *New York Times* (February 5, 2013), p. A24. Also see the tortured and confused defense of procedure by Brooks in David Brooks, "Florence and the Drones," *New York Times* (February 7, 201), p. A27.

21. Tom Engelhardt, "The American Lockdown State," *TomDispatch* (February 5, 2013). Online: http://www.tomdispatch.com/post/175646/tomgram%3A_engelhardt%2C_paying_the_bin_laden_tax

22. Teddy Cruz, "Democratizing Urbanization and the Search for a New Civic Imagination," in Nato Thompson, ed., *Living as*

Form: Socially Engaged Art from 1991-2011 (New York: Creative Time Books, 2012), p. 57.

CHAPTER FIVE

1. Eduardo Galeano, "The Theatre of Good and Evil," *La Jornada* (September 21, 2001), translated by Justin Podur.

2. Andrew O'Hehir, "How Boston Exposes America's Dark Post-9/11 Bargain," *Salon* (April 20, 2013). Online: http://www.salon.com/2013/04/20/how_boston_exposes_americas_dark_post_911_bargain

3. Zygmunt Bauman, *In Search of Politics* (Stanford: Stanford University Press, 1999), p. 13.

4. Michael Schwalbe, "The Lockdown Society Goes Primetime," *CounterPunch* (April 24, 2013). Online: http://www.counterpunch.org/2013/04/24/the-lockdown-society-goes-primetime/. See also Josh Gerstein and Darren Samuelsohn, "Boston Lockdown: The New Normal?" *Politico* (April 20, 2013), online: http://www.politico.com/story/2013/04/boston-bombing-lockdown-suspect-search-90364_Page2.html; and Wendy Kaminer, "'We Don't Cower in Fear': Reconsidering the Boston Lockdown," *The Atlantic* (April 21, 2013), online: http://www.theatlantic.com/national/archive/2013/04/we-don't-cower-in-fear-reconsidering-the-boston-lockdown/275165

5. Steven Rosenfeld, "America's Focus on Terrorism Blinds Us to Everyday Violence and Suffering," *AlterNet* (April 22, 2013). Online: http://www.alternet.org/americas-focus-terrorism-blinds-us-everyday-violence-and-suffering

6. I want to thank Professor Keith Tester for this point. Personal correspondence, May 8, 2013.

7. Guy Standing, *The Precariat: A Dangerous Class* (New York: Bloomsbury, 2011), p. 132.

8. David Oshinsky, "In the Heart of the Heat of Conspiracy," *New York Times Sunday Book Review* (January 27, 2008). Online: http://www.nytimes.com/2008/01/27/books/review/Oshinsky-t.html?_r=2&8bu=&oref=slogin&emc=bu&pagewanted=print&

9. William Rivers Pitt, "Random Notes from the Police State,"

Truthout (April 23, 2013). Online: http://truth-out.org/opinion/item/15895-random-notes-from-the-police-state

10. On the cost of American militarism and national security, see Melvin R. Goodman, *National Insecurity: the Cost of American Militarism* (San Francisco: City Lights, 2013).

11. Igor Volsky, "Top Opponent of Immigration Reform Totally Loses It During Immigration Hearing," *ThinkProgress* (April 22, 2013). Online: http://thinkprogress.org/immigration/2013/04/22/1901611/top-opponent-of-immigration-reform-totally-loses-it-during-immigration-hearing

12. On the question of racism and the response to the Boston Marathon bombing, see David Sirota, "The Huge, Unanswered Questions Post-Boston," *Salon* (April 21, 2013), online: http://www.salon.com/2013/04/21/the_huge_unanswered_questions_post_boston/; and Andrew O'Hehir, "How Boston Exposes America's Dark Post-9/11 Bargain," *Salon* (April 20, 2013), online: http://www.salon.com/2013/04/20/how_boston_exposes_americas_dark_post_911_bargain

13. Adam Serwer, "5 of the Worst Reactions to the Boston Manhunt," *Mother Jones* (April 19, 2013). Online: http://www.motherjones.com/mojo/2013/04/five-worst-reactions-boston-manhunt. Some critics argued persuasively that the government response to the Boston marathon bombing indicated the degree to which the surveillance state failed. See John Stanton, "US National Security State Fails in Boston," *Dissident Voice* (April 20, 2013), online: http://dissidentvoice.org/2013/04/us-national-security-state-fails-in-boston; and Falguni A. Sheth and Robert E. Prasch, "In Boston, Our Bloated Surveillance State Didn't Work," *Salon* (April 22, 2013), online: http://www.salon.com/2013/04/22/in_boston_our_bloated_surveillance_state_didnt_work

14. Serwer, "5 of the Worst Reactions to the Boston Manhunt."

15. David A. Graham, "Shorter Lindsey Graham: Constitution? What Constitution?" *The Atlantic* (April 19, 2013). Online: shttp://www.theatlantic.com/politics/archive/2013/04/shorter-lindsey-graham-constitution-what-constitution/275157/

16. Ibid.

17. Ulrich Beck, "The Silence of Words and Political Dynamics in the World Risk Society," *Logos* 1: 4 (Fall 2002), p. 9.

18. Katie McDonough, "New York State Senator on Boston Suspect: 'Who Wouldn't Use Torture on this Punk?'" *Salon* (April 20, 2013). Online: http://www.salon.com/2013/04/20/new_york_state_senator_on_boston_suspect_who_wouldnt_use_torture_on_this_punk

19. Report by the American Civil Liberties Union of Ohio, *How Ohio's Debtors' Prisons Are Ruining Lives and Costing Communities* (Cleveland: ACLU, 2013). Online: http://www.acluohio.org/wp-content/uploads/2013/04/TheOutskirtsOfHope2013_04.pdf

20. Hannah Groch-Begley, "Fox Asks if Children Should Work for School Meals," *Media Matters* (April 25, 2013). Online: http://mediamatters.org/mobile/blog/2013/04/25/fox-asks-if-children-should-work-for-school-mea/193768

21. See Annette Fuentes, *Lockdown High: When the Schoolhouse Becomes a Jailhouse* (New York: Verso, 2011); and Erik Eckholm, "With Police in Schools, More Children in Court," *New York Times* (April 12, 2013). Online: http://www.nytimes.com/2013/04/12/education/with-police-in-schools-more-children-in-court.html?ref=erikeckholm&_r=0

22. I am drawing from the excellent article by Jonathan Turley, "10 Reasons the U.S. Is No Longer the Land of the Free," *Washington Post* (January 13, 2012). Online: http://articles.washingtonpost.com/2012-01-13/opinions/35440628_1_individual-rights-indefinite-detention-citizens

23. Noam Chomsky, "Boston and Beyond: Terrorism at Home and Abroad," *In These Times* (March 13, 2013). Online: http://readersupportednews.org/opinion2/277-75/17259-boston-and-beyond-terrorism-at-home-and-abroad

24. Tom Engelhardt, "The American Lockdown State," *Tom Dispatch* (February 5, 2013). Online: http://www.tomdispatch.com/blog/175646

25. Cited in Bill Moyers, "The Boston Manhunt as a 'Political' Event," *Truthout* (April 25, 2013). Online: http://truth-out.org/news/item/16007-the-boston-manhunt-as-a-political-event

26. One of the few who provided this type of analysis was

Michael Schwalbe, "The Lockdown Society Goes Primetime," *CounterPunch* (April 24, 2013). Online: http://www.counterpunch.org/2013/04/24/the-lockdown-society-goes-primetime

27. Jennifer Rubin, "Sen. Lindsey Graham: Boston Bombing 'Is Exhibit A of Why the Homeland Is the Battlefield,'" *Washington Post* (April 19, 2013). Online: http://www.washingtonpost.com/blogs/right-turn/wp/2013/04/19/sen-lindsey-graham-boston-bombing-is-exhibit-a-of-why-the-homeland-is-the-battlefield

28. Michael Cohen, "Why Does America Lose Its Head over 'Terror' but Ignores Its Daily Gun Deaths?" *The Guardian* (April 21, 2013). Online: http://www.guardian.co.uk/commentisfree/2013/apr/21/boston-marathon-bombs-us-gun-law/print

29. Jack Healy, In Age of School Shootings, Lockdown Is the New Fire Drill, *New York Times*, January 12, 2014. Accessed February 24, 2014: http://nyti.ms/1cvXF2v.

30. Guy Standing, *The Precariat: A Dangerous Class* (New York: Bloomsbury, 2011), p. 132.

31. A number of excellent sources address this issue. See, for example, James Bamford, *The Shadow Factory: The NSA from 9/11 to the Eavesdropping on America* (New York: Anchor Books, 2009); Zygmunt Bauman and David Lyons, *Liquid Surveillance: A Conversation* (London: Polity, 2013); Michael Hardt and Antonio Negri, *Declaration* (New York: Argo Navis Author Services, 2012). Relatedly, see Stephen Graham, *Cities under Siege: The New Military Urbanism* (New York: Verso, 2011).

32. Jonathan Simon, *Governing through Crime: How the War on Crime Transformed American Democracy and Created a Culture of Fear* (New York: Oxford University Press, 2009).

33. Nicole Flatow, "Report: Mississippi Children Handcuffed in School for Not Wearing a Belt," *Nation of Change* (January 18, 2013). Online: http://www.nationofchange.org/report-mississippi-children-handcuffed-school-not-wearing-belt-1358527224. See also Suzi Parker, "Cops Nab 5-Year-Old for Wearing Wrong Color Shoes to School," *Take Part* (January 18, 2013). Online: http://www.takepart.com/article/2013/01/18/cops-nab-five-year-old-wearing-wrong-color-shoes-school

34. Alex Kane, "Miss a Traffic Ticket, Go to Jail? The Return of Debtor Prison (Hard Times, USA)," *AlterNet* (February 3, 2013). Online: http://www.alternet.org/miss-traffic-ticket-go-jail-return-debtor-prison-hard-times-usa

35. Cited in Dick Price, "More Black Men Now in Prison System Than Were Enslaved," *LA Progressive* (March 31, 2011). Online: http://www.zcommunications.org/more-black-men-now-in-prison-system-than-enslaved-in-1850-by-dick-price

36. See, for instance, Robert Scheer, "277 Million Boston Bombings," *Truthdig* (April 23, 2013). Online: http://www.truthdig.com/report/item/277_million_boston_bombings_20130423/?ln

37. Zygmunt Bauman and Leonidas Donskis, *Moral Blindness: The Loss of Sensitivity in Liquid Modernity* (London: Polity, 2013), p. 7.

38. Kathy E. Ferguson and Phyllis Turnbull, *Oh, Say, Can You See? The Semiotics of the Military in Hawai'i* (Minnesota: University of Minnesota Press, 1999), p. 155.

39. Tom Engelhardt, "Washington's Militarized Mindset," *TomDispatch* (July 5, 2012). Online: http://www.tomdispatch.com/blog/175564

40. Tom Engelhardt, "The American Lockdown State," *TomDispatch* (February 5, 2013). Online: http://www.tomdispatch.com/blog/175646

41. Steven Rosenfeld, "What Is the Cause of Violent and Senseless Massacres in America?" *AlterNet* (July 24, 2012). Online: http://www.alternet.org/story/156415/what_is_the_cause_of_violent_and_senseless_massacres_in_america

42. Hardt and Negri, *Declaration*, p. 22.

43. Charles Derber and Yale Magrass, "When Wars Come Home," *Truthout* (February 19, 2013). Online: http://www.truth-out.org/opinion/item/14539-when-wars-come-home

44. Ulrich Beck, *The Reinvention of Politics* (Cambridge: Polity Press, 1999), p. 78.

45. Engelhardt, "The American Lockdown State."

46. Noam Chomsky, "Security and State Power," *Truthout* (March 3, 2014). Online: http://www.truth-out.org/opinion/item/22221-noam-chomsky-security-and-state-power

47. Huntington cited in Jim Hunt, *They Said What?: Astonishing Quotes on American Democracy, Power, and Dissent* (Sausalito CA, Polipoint Press, 2009), p. 8.

48. Brian Terrell, "Drones, Sanctions, and the Prison Industrial Complex," *Monthly Review Magazine* (April 24, 2013). Online: http://mrzine.monthlyreview.org/2013/terrell240413.html

49. See Mark Karlin, "How the Prison-Industrial Complex Destroys Lives: An Interview with Marc Mauer," *Truthout* (April 26, 2013). Online: http://www.truth-out.org/progressivepicks/item/16003-the-prison-industrial-complex-the-pac-man-that-destroys-lives. There are many excellent resources on the subject. See, for instance, Angela Y. Davis, *Abolition Democracy: Beyond Prisons, Torture, and Empire* (New York: Seven Stories, 2005); Marc Mauer, *Race to Incarcerate* (New York: New Press, 2006); Anne-Marie Cusac, *Cruel and Unusual: The Culture of Punishment in America* (New Haven: Yale University Press, 2009); and Michelle Alexander, *New Jim Crow: Mass Incarceration in the Age of Colorblindness* (New York: New Press, 2012).

50. Ethan Bronner, "Poor Land in Jail as Companies Add Huge Fees for Probation," *New York Times* (July 2, 2012), p. A1.

51. Bill Lichtenstein, "A Terrifying Way to Discipline Children," *New York Times* (September 8, 2012). Online: http://www.nytimes.com/2012/09/09/opinion/sunday/a-terrifying-way-to-discipline-children.html?_r=0

52. Ian Urbina and Catherine Rentz, "Immigrants Held in Solitary Cells, Often for Weeks," *New York Times* (March 23, 2013). Online: http://www.nytimes.com/2013/03/24/us/immigrants-held-in-solitary-cells-often-for-weeks.html?pagewanted=all

53. Barry Lando, "The Boston Marathon Bombing, Drones and the Meaning of Cowardice," *CounterPunch* (April 16, 2013). Online: http://www.counterpunch.org/2013/04/16/the-boston-marathon-bombing-drones-and-the-meaning-of-cowardice

54. Joshua Kurlantzick, *Democracy in Retreat* (New Haven: Yale University Press, 2013); and Hardt and Negri, *Declaration.*

55. Peter Edelman, *So Rich, So Poor: Why It's So Hard to End Poverty in America* (New York: The New Press, 2012); Joseph Stiglitz,

The Price of Inequality (New York: W. W. Norton, 2012). See also the brilliant article on inequality by Michael Yates, "The Great Inequality," *Monthly Review* (March 1, 2012). Online: http://monthlyreview. org/2012/03/01/the-great-inequality

56. Matt Taibbi, *Rolling Stone*, "Gangster Bankers: Too Big to Jail," February 28, 2013. Online: http://www.rollingstone.com/politics/news/gangster-bankers-too-big-to-jail-20130214

57. See Henry A. Giroux, *Youth in Revolt* (Boulder: Paradigm, 2013).

58. Salman Rushdie, "Wither Moral Courage," *New York Times* (April 27, 2013), p. SR5.

59. Noam Chomsky, *The Culture of Terrorism* (Boston: South End Press, 1988), p. 21.

60. Pierre Bourdieu, *Acts of Resistance* (New York: Free Press, 1998), p. 1.

61. Gayatri Chakravorty Spivak, "Changing Reflexes: Interview with Gayatri Chakravorty Spivak," *Works and Days* 28: 55/56 (2010), pp. 1–2.

62. Ulrich Beck, *Democracy without Enemies* (London: Polity Press, 1998), p. 38.

CHAPTER SIX

1. See, for example, David Harvey, *The New Imperialism* (New York: Oxford University Press, 2003); David Harvey, *A Brief History of Neoliberalism* (Oxford: Oxford University Press, 2005); Wendy Brown, *Edgework* (Princeton: Princeton University Press, 2005); Henry A. Giroux, *Against the Terror of Neoliberalism* (Boulder: Paradigm Publishers, 2008); and Manfred B. Steger and Ravi K. Roy, *Neoliberalism: A Very Short Introduction* (Oxford University Press, 2010).

2. Chris Maisano, "Chicken Soup for the Neoliberal Soul," *Jacobin*, (January 21, 2014). Online: https://www.jacobinmag.com/2014/01/chicken-soup-for-the-neoliberal-soul

3. Michael Halberstam, "Introduction," *Totalitarianism and the Modern Conception of Politics*, (Yale University Press, 1999), p. 2.

4. Leo Gerard, The Billionaires' Scheme to Destroy Democracy,

In These Times, Web only, February 15, 2014: http://inthesetimes.com/article/16341/the_billionaire_scheme_to_destroy_democracy

5. Allison LaFave, "5 Reasons Why You Should Be Willing to Risk Arrest to Protect Public Education," *AlterNet* (April 8, 2013). Online: http://www.alternet.org/education/5-reasons-why-you-should-be-willing-risk-arrest-protect-public-education

6. Curtis Black, "Planning Lags for Homeless Students," *Newstips by Curtis Black* (May 19, 2013). Online: http://www.newstips.org/2013/05/planning-lags-for-homeless-students/?utm_source=feedburner&utm_medium=email&utm_campaign=Feed%3A+communitymediaworkshop%2Fnewstips+%28Chicago+Newstips+by+Curtis+Black%29

7. Valerie Strauss, "Three Days of Marches in Chicago to Protest School Closings," *Washington Post* (May 17, 2013). Online: http://www.washingtonpost.com/blogs/answer-sheet/wp/2013/05/17/three-days-of-marches-in-chicago-to-protest-school-closings

8. Lauren McCauley, "Hundreds of Chicago Students Walk Out of Standardized Test," *CommonDreams* (April 24, 2013). Online: http://www.commondreams.org/headline/2013/04/24-8

9. On the issue of school violence and the politics of school closing, see Mark Konkol and Paul Biasco, "Parents Win Battle, Manierre Elementary Won't Close," *DNAInfo Chicago* (May 21, 2013).

10. Phil Rogers, "Chicago FOP Says Use of Firefighters Is Another Admission That CPD Is Understaffed," *NBCChicago* (May 13, 2013). Online: http://www.nbcchicago.com/investigations/chicago-fire-department-school-closures-safe-passage-207295461.html

11. Diane Ravitch cited in Amy Goodman, "Chicago to Shutter 50 Public Schools."

12. On the rise of the racist punishing state, see Michelle Alexander, *The New Jim Crow: Mass Incarceration in the Age of Colorblindness* (New York: The New Press, 2010). On the severe costs of massive inequality, Joseph E. Stiglitz, *The Price of Inequality: How Today's Divided Society Endangers Our Future* (New York: Norton, 2012). On the turning of public schools into prisons, see Annette Fuentes, *Lockdown High: When the Schoolhouse Becomes a Jailhouse* (New York:

Verso, 2011).

13. Peter Brogan, "What's Behind the Attack on Teachers and Public Education?" *Solidarity* (September 14, 2012). Online: http://www.solidarity-us.org/site/node/3700

14. Quoted in Michael L. Silk and David L. Andrews, "(Re)Presenting Baltimore: Place, Policy, Politics, and Cultural Pedagogy," *Review of Education, Pedagogy, and Cultural Studies* 33 (2011), p. 436.

15. Terry Eagleton, "Reappraisals: What Is the Worth of Social Democracy?" *Harper's Magazine* (October 2010), p. 78. Online: http://www.harpers.org/archive/2010/10/0083150

16. Alex Honneth, *Pathologies of Reason* (New York: Columbia University Press, 2009), p. 188.

17. For an excellent analysis of contemporary forms of neoliberalism, see Stuart Hall, "The Neo-Liberal Revolution," *Cultural Studies*, 25: 6 (November 2011), pp. 705–728. See also David Harvey, *A Brief History of Neoliberalism* (Oxford: Oxford University Press, 2005); and Henry A. Giroux, *Against the Terror of Neoliberalism* (Boulder: Paradigm Publishers, 2008).

18. Diane Ravitch, "Is There Any Organization Not Funded by Gates?" *Diane Ravitch's Blog* (May 9, 2013). Online: http://dianeravitch.net/2013/05/09/is-there-any-organization-that-is-not-funded-by-gates/. For an extensive analysis of this issue, see Kenneth Saltman, *The Failure of Corporate School Reform* (Boulder: Paradigm, 2012); and Philip Kovacs, ed., *The Gates Foundation and the Future of US "Public" Schools* (New York: Routledge, 2010).

19. For examples of this tradition, see Maria Nikolakaki, ed., *Critical Pedagogy in the Dark Ages: Challenges and Possibilities* (New York: Peter Lang, 2012) and Henry A. Giroux, *On Critical Pedagogy* (New York: Continuum, 2011).

20. Lauren McCauley, "Hundreds of Chicago Students Walk Out of Standardized Test," *CommonDreams* (April 24, 2013). Online: http://www.commondreams.org/headline/2013/04/24-8

21. "Teacher Boycott of Standardized Tests Wins Local, National Backing," *Democracy Now* (January 28, 2013). Online: http://www.democracynow.org/2013/1/28/headlines/teacher_boycott_of_standardized_tests_wins_local_national_backing

22. Amy Goodman, "Seattle Teachers, Students Win Historic Victory Over Standardized Testing," *Truthout* (May 20, 2013). Online: http://truth-out.org/news/item/16486-seattle-teachers-students-win-historic-victory-over-standardized-testing

23. See Henry A. Giroux, *The Education Deficit and the War on Youth* (New York: Monthly Review Press, 2013).

CHAPTER SEVEN

1. Tony Judt, "Tony Judt: 'I Am Not Pessimistic in the Very Long Run,'" *The Independent* (March 24, 2010). Online: http://www.independent.co.uk/arts-entertainment/books/features/tony-judt-i-am-not-pessimistic-in-the-very-long-run-1925966.html

2. David Theo Goldberg, "Mission Accomplished: Militarizing Social Logic," in Cuauhtémoc Medina, ed., *Enrique Jezik: Obstruct, Destroy, Conceal* (Mexico: Universidad Nacional Autónoma de México, 2011), pp. 183–198.

3. See, for example, Colin Leys, *Market Driven Politics* (London: Verso, 2001); Randy Martin, *Financialization of Daily Life* (Philadelphia: Temple University Press, 2002); Pierre Bourdieu, *Firing Back: Against the Tyranny of the Market 2*, trans. Loic Wacquant (New York: The New Press, 2003); Alfredo Saad-Filho and Deborah Johnston, *Neoliberalism: A Critical Reader* (London: Pluto Press, 2005); Henry A. Giroux, *Against the Terror of Neoliberalism* (Boulder: Paradigm, 2008); David Harvey, *A Brief History of Neoliberalism* (New York: Oxford University Press, 2007); Manfred B. Steger and Ravi K. Roy, *Neoliberalism: A Very Short Introduction* (New York: Oxford University Press, 2010); Gerad Dumenil and Dominique Levy, *The Crisis of Neoliberalism* (Cambridge: Harvard University Press, 2011). Henry A. Giroux, *Twilight of the Social* (Boulder: Paradigm, 2013); Stuart Hall, "The March of the Neoliberals," *The Guardian* (September 12, 2011), online: http://www.guardian.co.uk/politics/2011/sep/12/march-of-the-neoliberals

4. See, most recently, Kelly V. Vlahos, "Boots on Campus," *AntiWar.com* (February 26, 2013), online: http://original.antiwar.com/vlahos/2013/02/25/boots-on-campus/; and David H. Price, *Weaponizing Anthropology* (Oakland: AK Press, 2011).

5. Greg Bishop, "A Company That Runs Prisons Will Have Its Name on a Stadium," *New York Times* (February 19, 2013). Online: http://www.nytimes.com/2013/02/20/sports/ncaafootball/a-company-that-runs-prisons-will-have-its-name-on-a-stadium.html?_r=0

6. Goldberg, "Mission Accomplished," pp. 197–198.

7. Jonathan Schell, "Cruel America," *The Nation* (September 28, 2011). Online: http://www.thenation.com/article/163690/cruel-america

8. Suzi Parker, "Cops Nab 5-Year-Old for Wearing Wrong Color Shoes to School," *Take Part* (January 18, 2013). Online: http://www.takepart.com/article/2013/01/18/cops-nab-five-year-old-wearing-wrong-color-shoes-school

9. Susan Saulny, "After Recession, More Young Adults Are Living on Street," *New York Times* (December 18, 2012). Online: http://www.nytimes.com/2012/12/19/us/since-recession-more-young-americans-are-homeless.html?pagewanted=all&_r=0

10. Gretchen Morgenson, "A Loan Fraud War That's Short on Combat," *New York Times*, (March 15, 2014). Online: http://nyti.ms/1fzqhcJ

11. A. O. Scott, "Finding Comfort in Easy Distinctions," *New York Times* (February 28, 2013). Online: http://www.nytimes.com/interactive/2013/03/03/arts/critics-on-violence-in-media.html

12. Aaron Cantu, "'Do What You Gotta Do': Cop Shows Bolster Idea That Police Violence Works," *Truthout* (March 16, 2014). Online: http://www.truth-out.org/news/item/22433-do-what-you-gotta-do-cop-shows-bolster-idea-that-police-violence-works

13. Bethania Palma Markus, "Journalist Calls for Accountability in Police Killings," *Truthout* (March 18, 2014). Online: http://www.truth-out.org/news/item/22538-journalist-calls-for-accountability-in-police-killings

14. Editorial, "Introduction: Living with Death," *New York Times* (February 28, 2013). Online: http://www.nytimes.com/interactive/2013/03/03/arts/critics-on-violence-in-media.html

15. Suzanne Gamboa and Monika Mathur, "Guns Kill Young Children Daily in the U.S.," *Huffington Post* (December 24, 2012). Online: http://www.huffingtonpost.com/2012/12/24/guns-

children_n_2359661.html

16. Etienne Balibar, "Outline of a Topography of Cruelty: Citizenship and Civility in the Era of Global Violence," in *We, the People of Europe? Reflections on Transnational Citizenship* (Princeton: Princeton University Press, 2004), pp. 125–126.

17. John Le Carré, "The United States of America Has Gone Mad," *CommonDreams* (January 15, 2003). Online: http://www.commondreams.org/views03/0115-01.htm

18. Eric Mann interview with Mumia Abu Jamal, "Mumia Abu Jamal: On His Biggest Political Influences and the Political 'Mentacide' of Today's Youth," *Voices from the Frontlines Radio* (April 9, 2012). Online: http://www.thestrategycenter.org/radio/2012/09/04/mumia-abu-jamal-his-biggest-political-influences-and-political-mentacide-todays-you

19. See, for example, Charles Ferguson, *Predator Nation: Corporate Criminals, Political Corruption, and the Hijacking of America* (New York: Random House, 2012).

20. Michael Yates, "The Great Inequality," *Monthly Review* (March 1, 2012). Online: http://monthlyreview.org/2012/03/01/the-great-inequality

21. Ibid.

22. Julie Creswell, "Hedge Fund Titans' Pay Stretching to 10 Figures," *New York Times* (April 15, 2013). Online: http://dealbook.nytimes.com/2013/04/15/pay-stretching-to-10-figures

23. Paul Bucheitt, "4 Ways the Koch Brothers' Wealth Is Beyond Comprehension," *Alternet* (November 24, 2013). Online: http://www.alternet.org/economy/4-ways-koch-brothers-wealth-beyond-comprehension

24. Paul Buchheit, "Five Ugly Extremes of Inequality in America—The Contrasts Will Drop Your Chin to the Floor," *AlterNet* (March 24, 2013). Online: http://www.alternet.org/economy/five-ugly-extremes-inequality-america-contrasts-will-drop-your-chin-floor

25. Ibid. Paul Buchheit, "4 Ways the Koch Brothers' Wealth Is Beyond Comprehension."

26. Guy Standing, *The New Precariat: The New Dangerous Class* (New York: Bloomsbury, 2011).

27. Zygmunt Bauman, *Liquid Times: Living in an Age of Uncertainty* (Cambridge: Polity Press, 2007).

28. This issue is taken up brilliantly in Irving Howe, "Reaganism: The Spirit of the Times," *Selected Writings 1950–1990* (New York: Harcourt Brace Jovanovich, 1990), pp. 410–423.

29. I address this issue in detail in Henry A. Giroux, *The University in Chains: Challenging the Military-Industrial-Academic Complex* (Boulder: Paradigm, 2007).

30. Aaron B. O'Connell, "The Permanent Militarization of America," *New York Times* (November 4, 2012). Online: http://www.nytimes.com/2012/11/05/opinion/the-permanent-militarization-of-america.html?pagewanted=all&_r=0

31. Dominic Tierney, "The F-35: A Weapon That Costs More Than Australia," *The Atlantic* (February 13, 2013). Online: http://www.theatlantic.com/national/archive/2011/03/the-f-35-a-weapon-that-costs-more-than-australia/72454

32. Chase Madar, "The School Security America Doesn't Need," *TomDispatch* (February 26, 2013). Online: http://www.tomdispatch.com/post/175654/tomgram%3A_chase_madar%2C_handcuffing_seven-year-olds_won%27t_make_schools_safer/?utm_source=TomDispatch&utm_campaign=ee150a2906-TD_Madar2_26_2013&utm_medium=email. These issues have been examined extensively in Henry A. Giroux, *Youth in a Suspect Society* (New York: Palgrave, 2009); Christopher Robbins, *Expelling Hope: The Assault on Youth and the Militarization of Schooling* (New York: SUNY Press, 2008); and Annette Fuentes, *Lockdown High* (New York: Verso, 2011).

33. John Hinkson, "The GFC Has Just Begun," *Arena Magazine* no. 122 (March 2013), p. 51.

34. John Atcheson, "Dark Ages Redux: American Politics and the End of the Enlightenment," *CommonDreams* (June 18, 2012). Online: https://www.commondreams.org/view/2012/06/18-2

35. Mark Slouka, "A Quibble," *Harper's Magazine* (February 2009). Online: http://www.harpers.org/archive/2009/02/0082362

36. Stanley Aronowitz, Rick Wolfe, et al., *Manifesto, Left Turn: An Open Letter to U.S. Radicals* (New York: The Fifteenth Street

Manifesto Group, March 2008), pp. 4–5.

37. Martin Luther King Jr., "Letter from Birmingham City Jail (1963)," in James M. Washington, ed., *The Essential Writings and Speeches of Martin Luther King, Jr.* (New York: Harper Collins, 1991), pp. 290, 298.

38. Ibid, p. 296.

39. James Baldwin, "An Open Letter to My Sister, Miss Angela Davis," *New York Review of Books* (January 7, 1971). Online: http://www.nybooks.com/articles/archives/1971/jan/07/an-open-letter-to-my-sister-miss-angela-davis/?pagination=false

40. James B. Conant, "Wanted: American Radicals," *The Atlantic* (May 1943). Online: http://www.theatlantic.com/issues/95sep/ets/radical.htm

41. Steve Herbert and Elizabeth Brown, "Conceptions of Space and Crime in the Punitive Neoliberal City," *Antipode* 38: 4 (2006), p. 757.

42. Henry A. Giroux, *Education and the Crisis of Public Values* (New York: Peter Lang, 2013); and Henry A. Giroux, *The Education Deficit and the War on Youth* (New York: Monthly Review Press, 2013).

43. Hass cited in Sarah Pollock, "Robert Hass," *Mother Jones* (March–April 1992), p. 22

44. Robin Kelley, "Foreword," in Angela Y. Davis, *The Meaning of Freedom* (San Francisco: City Lights, 2012), pp. 7–16.

45. Paul Buchheit, "Five Ugly Extremes of Inequality in America—The Contrasts Will Drop Your Chin to the Floor," *Alternet* (March 24, 2013). Online: http://www.alternet.org/economy/five-ugly-extremes-inequality-america-contrasts-will-drop-your-chin-floor

46. Angela Y. Davis, *Abolition Democracy: Beyond Empire, Prisons, and Torture* (New York: Seven Stories Press, 2005), pp. 72–73.

CHAPTER EIGHT

1. Robert Reich, "Breakfast with My Mentor," *Reader Supported News* (August 29, 2013), http://readersupportednews.org/opinion2/275-42/19134-focus-breakfast-with-my-mentor

2. Doreen Massey, "Vocabularies of the Economy," *Soundings*,

(2013). Online: http://lwbooks.co.uk/journals/soundings/pdfs/Vo-cabularies%20of%20the%20economy.pdf

3. Stuart Hall, "The Kilburn Manifesto: Our Challenge to the Neoliberal Victory," *Common Dreams* (April 24, 2013). Online: https://www.commondreams.org/view/2013/04/24-10

4. ACLU Comment on Bradley Manning Sentence, ACLU (August 21, 2013). Online: https://www.aclu.org/free-speech/aclu-comment-bradley-manning-sentence

5. Zygmunt Bauman, Globalization: The Human Consequences (New York: Columbia University Press, 1998), p. 5.

6. Paul Buchheit, "Five Facts That Put America to Shame," *Common Dreams* (May 14, 2012). Online: http://www.common-dreams.org/view/2012/05/14-0

7. There are too many sources to cite on this issue, but one is particularly important. See Michael Yates, "The Great Inequality," *Monthly Review*, (March 1, 2012) http://monthlyreview.org/2012/03/01/the-great-inequality

8. Paul Buchheit, "Five Ugly Extremes of Inequality in America—The Contrasts Will Drop Your Chin to the Floor," *Alternet*, (March 24, 2013). Online: http://www.alternet.org/economy/five-ugly-extremes-inequality-america-contrasts-will-drop-your-chin-floor

9. Robert Reich, "Republican Myth: Obama's 'Entitlement Society'," Robert Reich's Blog (February 21, 2012). Online: http://robertreich.org/post/16889736226

10. Zygmunt Bauman and David Lyon, *Liquid Surveillance*: *A Conversation* (Cambridge, UK: Polity Press, 2013), p. 147.

11. Stanley Aronowitz, "Where is the Outrage," *Situations* 5: 2 (2014), p. 37.

12. Ibid., p. 37.

13. Andrew Benjamin, *Present Hope: Philosophy, Architecture, Ju-daism* (New York: Routledge, 1997), p. 1.

14. Bloch's great contribution in English on the subject of utopi-anism can be found in his three-volume work, Ernst Bloch, *The Principle of Hope*, trans. Neville Plaice, Stephen Plaice and Paul Knight (Cambridge: MIT Press, 1986, originally published in 1959).

15. Ernst Block, "Something's Missing: A Discussion Between

Ernst Bloch and Theodor W. Adorno on the Contradictions of Utopia Longing," in Ernst Bloch, *The Utopian Function of Art and Literature: Selected Essays* (Cambridge, MA: MIT Press, 1988), p. 3.

16. Robert Jensen, "With Truce at the UT Factory, Time to Face Tough Choices," *Truthout* (September 6, 2013). Online: http://www.truth-out.org/opinion/item/18650-with-truce-at-the-ut-factory-time-to-face-tough-choices

17. Robin D. G. Kelley, "Empire State of Mind," *CounterPunch*, (August 16, 2013). Online: http://www.counterpunch.org/2013/08/16/empire-state-of-mind/print.

18. Ibid., Aronowitz, "Where Is the Outrage," *Situations* 5: 2(2014), p. 37.

19. Thomas L. Dunn, "A Political Theory for Losers," in Jason A. Frank and John Tambornino, eds. *Vocations of Political Theory* (Minneapolis: University of Minnesota Press, 2000), p. 160.

20. Cited in Zygmunt Bauman, *Work, Consumerism and the New Poor* (Philadelphia: Open University Press, 1998), p. 98.

21. Ron Aronson, "Hope after Hope?," *Social Research* 66: 2 (Summer 1999), p. 489.

22. Ibid., Aronowitz, "Where Is the Outrage," *Situations* 5: 2 (2014), p. 28.

23. Cited in Gary A. Olson and Lynn Worsham, "Changing the Subject: Judith Butler's Politics of Radical Resignification," JAC 20:4 (2000), p. 765.

24. Ibid.

25. Ibid., Aronowitz, "Where Is the Outrage," *Situations* 5: 2 (2014), p. 44.

26. Bauman and Lyon, *Liquid Surveillance: A Conversation*, p. 159.

INDEX

"Passim" (literally "scattered") indicates intermittent discussion of a topic over a cluster of pages.

Henry A. Giroux is a world-renowned educator, author, and public intellectual. He currently holds the McMaster University Chair for Scholarship in the Public Interest at McMaster University in the English and Cultural Studies Department. Giroux's most recent books include: *Zombie Politics and Culture in the Age of Casino Capitalism* (Peter Lang, 2011); *Henry Giroux on Critical Pedagogy* (Continuum, 2011); *Education and the Crisis of Public Values* (Peter Lang 2012); *Twilight of the Social: Resurgent Publics in the Age of Disposability* (Paradigm Publishers, 2012); *Disposable Youth* (Routledge 2012); *Youth in Revolt* (Paradigm, 2013); *The Education Deficit and the War on Youth* (Monthly Review Press, 2013); and *Neoliberalism's War on Higher Education* (Haymarket, 2014). A prolific writer and political commentator, he writes regularly for Truthout and serves on their board of directors. He currently lives in Hamilton, Ontario, Canada with his wife, Dr. Susan Searls Giroux.